how to be a great dad

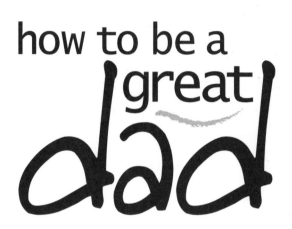

ian bruce

Foreword by
Dr. Alan Bradley,
Consultant Clinical Psychologist

foulsham
LONDON • NEW YORK • TORONTO • SYDNEY

foulsham

The Publishing House, Bennetts Close, Cippenham, Slough,
Berkshire, SL1 5AP, England

ISBN 0-572-03134-3

Copyright © 2005 Ian Bruce

Cover photograph © Powerstock

A CIP record for this book is available from the British Library

The moral right of the author has been asserted

Printed in Great Britain by Creative Print and Design (Wales), Ebbw Vale

Contents

Foreword

Being a parent is the hardest job in the world. Being a 'great' parent would appear to be impossible!

However, in writing *How to Be a Great Dad,* Ian Bruce has not only produced a thoughtful and very comprehensive insight into what it is to be a dad at the beginning of the twenty-first century, but has done so in a very accessible manner.

Ian has avoided the pitfalls of jargon and 'psychobabble', but by the use of everyday language has succeeded in transforming complex ideas into practical plans of action which we dads can incorporate into our everyday parenting.

By demystifying the idea of 'parenting' and simply stating that how to be a great dad is a set of skills that can be learned, Ian gives hope to all us dads who have simply been getting by somehow.

As a man who has been a parent for some thirty-four years now, and a Child and Family Clinical Psychologist for almost twenty years, I would recommend this book to the experienced dad, to the new dad, and indeed anyone who hopes to be a dad at some time in the future.

Dr Alan Bradley
Consultant Clinical Psychologist

Introduction

Let's be honest from the outset: *most men hate mediocrity.* We're competitive animals. We get huge amounts of satisfaction from doing things bigger, better, more efficiently, more effectively and with more enthusiasm. That's just the way we are built. And it's something to be thankful for. This basic desire to be great, rather than settle for mediocrity, has given us so much that we are proud of in the modern world. It gave us the industrial revolution, it put men on the moon and it flies us from London to New York in six hours. It gave us success in sport, the arts and in business the world over.

And now that same inner drive is spurring us on to become great dads.

A century ago, the idea of being a great dad would have sounded alien to most men. Back then, the role of the father involved little more than being a breadwinner and disciplinarian. As long as you were bringing home the bacon and could sternly reprimand the kids whenever they went astray, you could spend the rest of the time tucked away in your private study and you'd still be considered a fairly good father.

But times have changed, and our role as fathers today is very different from what it used to be. Fatherhood in the twenty-first century involves not only bringing home the bacon and being stern when that's appropriate, but many other things that were once considered the primary domain of women. The modern dad is expected to be able to cover all bases, acting as a coach, carer, counsellor, educator, encourager, entertainer, manager, motivator, nurse, nutritionist, safety officer ... and the list goes on and on.

This much more expanded role of being a father in the modern world is tremendously exciting. It gives us a chance to be far more involved with our children than at any other time in history. But at the same time, it can also be very challenging – especially if we want to do a great job instead of just an average one.

How to Be a Great Dad is my response to this challenge. As the title suggests, it's a complete guide to being a great dad for your child – from the moment of conception right through to adulthood. Of course, your journey as a father will still have its ups and downs, and you will still make some mistakes, but using this guide will help ensure that your predominant mode is one of greatness.

Greatness is a high level of skill which is gained through a combination of both education and experience. In order to become a great driver, you need to know the theory of driving, but you also need to spend plenty of time behind the wheel putting that theoretical knowledge into practice. The same applies to fatherhood. To become a great dad, you need to know the theory of being a great dad, but you also need to spend time applying that theoretical knowledge to the relationships you have with your kids.

This book will provide the vital education you need to become a great dad, but only you can take the information it contains and use it to become a great dad in reality. Simply reading this book might interest you for a few hours – and I hope it does – but if you actually strive to apply what you learn to your everyday relationships with your children then the reality of being a great dad will be something that you can enjoy for a lifetime.

Enjoy the journey!

CHAPTER 1

What Is a Great Dad?

You should note right at the start that the title of this book is *How to Be a Great Dad,* and not *How to Be a Perfect Dad.* Being great is an achievable 'process' goal, like being a great businessman, lover or golfer. The more you strive to attain this goal, the greater you'll become. And the best part is, no matter how great you already are, there's always room for further improvement.

Being perfect, by comparison, isn't an achievable goal, because no matter how hard you try, you'll never reach a point where you can sit back and say, 'I'm perfect.' To be perfect you would have to be able to please all of the people all of the time and live the rest of your life without making a single mistake, and that just isn't possible.

So right now, forget any notion that this book requires you to be perfect, because it doesn't. It only requires you to be great. Which brings us to the really important question: *What exactly does it mean to be a great dad?*

Key traits of paternal greatness

I have carried out a number of straw polls, and I can tell you that there are literally hundreds of possible responses to this question, but almost all of them can be grouped into what I call the Eight Key Traits of Paternal Greatness.

Key 1: The great dad gives unconditional love

The great dad is someone who loves his kids unconditionally. This means all the time, come hell or high water. He loves his kids when they're behaving and when they're misbehaving. He loves them when they throw up on the back seat of his brand-new car. He loves them when they spill milk on his computer keyboard. He loves them when they then grab his most expensive dress shirt from the laundry to wipe up the mess. He loves them when they make mistakes in their teenage years, when they cost him more money than he expected and when they tell him that they disagree with his opinion.

The great dad loves his kids – period.

Of course, this doesn't mean that the great dad never gets angry with his kids or frustrated with their behaviour, because he does. But no matter how his emotions fluctuate, his fundamental love for his children never wavers. It is solid, unstoppable and unconditional.

Key 2: The great dad communicates openly

The great dad communicates openly with his kids. He asks how they are feeling and encourages them to talk with him about their problems and challenges as well as their successes and achievements. He listens carefully to make sure that he understands their point of view, and he respects that point of view, even if it differs from his own.

As well as listening, the great dad talks. He doesn't expect his kids to simply know that he loves them, he tells them. If he asks his kids to do something, or refuses one of their requests, he explains why he has done those things. This is not because he necessarily needs to justify his reasoning, but because he wants them to understand that – even though they may not like his approach in the short term – he has their long-term best interests at heart.

He recognises that open communication is a two-way street, and he is willing to share his point of view with his kids in an appropriate way.

Key 3: The great dad spends time with his kids

Good dads are giving dads, but only great dads realise that time is the best gift of all. The great dad understands that he needs to give his kids time and attention so that their relationship can grow and flourish. If this essential time and attention isn't given then that same relationship will wither and die.

Some dads try to 'buy off' their kids by giving money, toys, clothes, trips, and so on, instead of their time – but all this does is make such fathers feel a little less guilty. None of this giving of tangible items means a thing if the one essential gift – time and attention – is withheld.

Now it's obvious that most of us lead busy lives. We have career responsibilities, personal responsibilities and a myriad of miscellaneous obligations which all require big chunks of our time. Great dads are just as busy as anyone else, yet they still find time to give to their kids.

The main hallmark of a great dad in this area is that he makes his children a top priority in his life. He schedules regular 'time with kids' in his appointments diary – and then he keeps that appointment as if his life depends on it.

Key 4: The great dad is patient

Great dads are patient dads. They realise that all children make mistakes, so they don't fly off the handle whenever this truth happens to show itself in daily life. Instead, they give their kids the time they need to learn and grow, all the while offering support and encouragement.

You might think that this kind of patience will mean that you end up waiting a lot longer for your child to complete a task, but usually the opposite is the case. Most kids make more mistakes when trying to rush through with something for an impatient father than they do when allowed the time to do things at their own pace. Paradoxically, being patient can therefore save more time than being impatient – and even if it doesn't, it will certainly have a positive impact on your child.

Key 5: The great dad sets a great example

Whether you like it or not, you are the first person your children will look up to as a role model of what a man should be like in the world. This puts a tremendous amount of responsibility on your shoulders, because the way you speak, the way you behave and the things that you do will all have a dramatic impact on the way your kids develop.

All of this means that you need to set the kind of example you will be happy for them to follow in the future. In other words, if you don't want them to become couch potatoes, you shouldn't spend six hours each evening watching TV yourself. And if you do want them to learn to eat their vegetables, you have to do that yourself. Unfortunately, French fries don't count.

Another important reason why you need to set a great example is because all kids hate hypocrisy. If there's ever any incongruence between what you say and what you do, rest assured that they will pay more attention to what you do. That's why great dads make a point of leading by example, and of letting their walk do the talk.

Key 6: The great dad knows how to have fun

The number one priority for most children is to squeeze as much fun from each day as they possibly can. This means that they relate well to others who know how to have fun. If you can be one of those people, you'll find that your relationship with your kids flourishes, and that they will see you as a human being in your own right, and not just as a 'dad'.

Of course, your idea of fun and your kids' idea of fun are probably two different things. To you, fun might mean a round of golf, or taking in the latest Vin Diesel movie. But to your kids, having fun is more likely to mean playing a computer games console, flying a kite or going swimming on a Saturday morning.

The idea here is not for you to have fun doing one thing whilst your kids have fun doing something else, but for you to join your kids and do what they enjoy. This might mean that you have to go swimming instead of golfing on a Saturday morning, or play a video game in the evening after work instead of reading the newspaper – but if you make these small adjustments, your kids will appreciate it more than you will ever know.

Obviously, when you do any of this you have to really throw yourself into it. Kids are enthusiastic creatures, and if you can't be equally enthusiastic whilst having fun with them, you'll only make yourself and everyone else miserable. So, for the hour or couple of hours you set aside to have fun, forget what you could be doing elsewhere and focus on enjoying the activity itself. By doing this, you'll be giving your kids some great memories which they will one day look back on with a lot of fondness.

Key 7: The great dad provides for his children

Your kids have needs, and until they are adults themselves it is your responsibility to meet those needs to the very best of your ability. Great dads know this, and work hard and effectively to ensure that they are able to provide for their children properly.

Note here that we are talking about providing for *needs*. That doesn't necessarily mean giving your kids everything that they *want*. For example, your kids will need a new pair of good-quality training shoes every now and again, but they probably won't need a £299 pair with gold-leaf go-faster stripes down the side. Helping your child to understand the difference between needs and wants is part of being a great dad, but then so is the willingness to provide for their real needs.

Key 8: The great dad is committed to greatness

The final key trait of great dads is that they never rest on their laurels. At no point do they ever sit back and think, 'I'm a great dad. That's it. My work is done.'

The truly great dad is committed to greatness, not just in parenthood, but in all other areas of his life too. It's part of who he is as a human being. He views each day as a brand-new opportunity to improve himself and his life in some way. He never affords himself the luxury of complacency.

This kind of attitude is something that kids pick up on quickly. If they see that you are committed to greatness, the chances are that they will adopt that same approach to life. As you can imagine, this will have a big impact on the way your child grows and matures, as well as on what he or she comes to achieve in life. So start as you mean to go on, and be committed to greatness.

These Eight Key Traits of Paternal Greatness are not absolutely definitive. There are undoubtedly several other traits that could also have been included. What does being a great dad mean to you personally? When you think of the phrase 'great dad', what kind of feelings, images and ideas does it suggest to you? If you find you have ideas that aren't covered by any of the eight key traits outlined above, create your own key trait which meets your own definition of the term. Then, once you have a list of key traits you are comfortable with, start living by them.

Many of the ideas touched upon here will be considered in more detail later – but for now, make a start. Start living by the traits you have listed and you'll soon notice the difference it makes to your life.

Why being a great dad is essential

I never like to focus on the negative side of life, but for a few moments I simply have to in order to get an important point across. Your kids are going to grow up in what can be a very dangerous world. There are people in this world who think it's normal when a teenager is addicted to crack or heroin. There are people in this world who think it's normal when a fourteen-year-old girl gets pregnant. There are people in this world who think it's normal when a twelve-year-old boy starts drinking alcohol on a regular basis. And the sad part of all this is that, in some social circles, all of these things are normal, or at least commonplace enough to be considered normal.

How can we protect our kids in a world like this? Well, there are two options. One is to give up the day job and provide 24-hour bodyguard services until our kids reach full maturity. Unfortunately, this option isn't really viable. Even if it were, our kids would hate the idea, since it would take away one of the most valuable things in life – freedom. So that leaves us with the only other option – becoming a great dad.

If you are a great dad, and you live by the traits outlined earlier, you will raise kids who are confident, think things through, aspire to greatness themselves and are willing to communicate with you openly about whatever they want. This makes them far less likely to blindly follow the example or advice of others, and therefore reduces the chances of them acting in a self-destructive manner.

Of course, I'm not saying that being a great dad is an absolute guarantee that our kids will never take drugs, drink alcohol underage or get pregnant, because the reality is that all of these things can occur regardless of parenting skills. However, I do maintain that the *chances* of our kids making these kinds of irrational choices are much reduced when the principles of being a great dad have been adhered to.

So the first reason why it's essential to be a great dad is because it reduces the chances of your kids getting into trouble later on. But there's also another very good reason for becoming a great dad – and that is because it's something that automatically makes you a better man.

You see, the principles of becoming a great dad are often principles that bring about simultaneous benefits in all the other areas of our lives. For example, by learning to be more patient and communicative in our relationship with our kids, we will automatically begin to use those skills in other important relationships with partners, friends and colleagues. Similarly, by learning to manage our time more effectively so that we can spend regular hours with our kids, the exact same discipline will automatically make us more effective at work. And there are many other ways in which our 'great dad habits' will have a beneficial impact on the non-parenting aspects of our lives.

Deciding to become a great dad is therefore deciding to become a great man in general.

SUMMARY OF CHAPTER 1

- Being a great dad does not mean being a perfect dad.
- There are Eight Key Traits of Paternal Greatness:
  - Key 1: The great dad gives unconditional love.
  - Key 2: The great dad communicates openly.
  - Key 3: The great dad spends time with his kids.
  - Key 4: The great dad is patient.
  - Key 5: The great dad sets a great example.
  - Key 6: The great dad knows how to have fun.
  - Key 7: The great dad provides for his children.
  - Key 8: The great dad is committed to greatness.
- Becoming a great dad will reduce the chances of your kids getting into trouble.
- Becoming a great dad automatically makes you a better man.

CHAPTER 2

It Starts with a Positive

M ost men think that the role of being a dad begins as soon as their first baby is born – but they are wrong. The role of being a great dad begins as soon as you find out that your partner is expecting your child, and that means that it all starts with a positive pregnancy test. From this point on you're a dad, so you need to know what to do as a dad between now and the day your child is born. Let's start by looking at the stages of pregnancy itself, and how it will impact on your relationship with your partner.

The trimesters

For purposes of discussion, pregnancy is generally divided into three main stages, called trimesters. The first trimester covers approximately the first fourteen weeks of pregnancy and, for many women, is the most challenging. This is because the physical system goes through some dramatic changes as it adjusts to the growing baby within it.

During this first trimester you can expect your partner to feel tired, nauseated (this should have ended by the end of the trimester), emotionally stressed and weepy – all due to hormonal changes taking place. She may also suffer from cramps, constipation, haemorrhoids and, in some cases, varicose veins. In addition to all of this, her breasts will begin to enlarge and will continue to do so (though not at a uniform rate) throughout the whole of the pregnancy.

The second trimester runs from around week fifteen to week twenty-seven. During this phase of the pregnancy your partner will gain weight and her abdomen will expand to accommodate the growing baby. Because her body has more weight to carry around, she may begin to experience aches and pains. Some symptoms that may have started in the first trimester, such as constipation, may continue.

The silver lining in all of this is that your baby will probably start kicking before the end of the second trimester. This is usually a very happy occasion, because that's when it will occur to both your partner and yourself that she's having a baby. Yes, you both already knew it intellectually. But when that baby gives her a kick – as if to say, 'Hey, it's me!' – the reality of the situation will suddenly hit home on a much deeper level.

The third trimester runs from around week twenty-eight until week forty, when she can expect to go into labour and give birth. Your partner will continue getting bigger as your baby grows, and any swelling or haemorrhoids that are already present could get marginally worse. Visits to the bathroom may also become more frequent, and your partner might experience shortness of breath as the weight of the baby puts increased pressure on her internal organs. Her breasts will probably become tender as they enlarge more rapidly towards the end of the pregnancy. In the final ten weeks of pregnancy, your partner may begin to experience irregular uterine contractions known as Braxton Hicks contractions. These are the body's way of getting geared up for the real thing when the time comes, and are perfectly normal, though they can be uncomfortable.

As you can see, pregnancy is no picnic. Of course, it's not all bad news for the entire duration by any means, but understanding all of these negative 'side-effects' of pregnancy will help you to exercise more patience during this sometimes difficult time. If you need a mantra to help you through, just remind yourself that pregnancy doesn't last forever – and at least you're only suffering from the symptoms indirectly.

Understanding what she's going through – I

Men sometimes complain that they can't understand why women moan so much during pregnancy, and therefore find it hard to be as compassionate as they feel they should be. Well, just think of it this way:

Although you eat well and get plenty of rest, you find yourself waking up with the uncontrollable urge to vomit. It feels like you've got a stomach bug of some sort, but in this case vomiting brings only temporary relief. You might feel just as nauseous during the middle of the day, and again in the early evening. Nobody knows when the urge to vomit will strike – least of all you.

Your moods start changing from good to bad and back again faster than you ever thought possible, and for no apparent reason. Things that you used to laugh about now bug the hell out of you, and tasks you used to cope with easily can now reduce you to tears.

You've always been conscious of your body, and you like to look good. But although you haven't changed any of your healthy habits, your body has started growing at a tremendous rate, and hardly a week goes by without the bathroom scales giving you the proof. Not that you need it. You often feel exhausted just climbing a flight of stairs.

But here's the clincher: there's nothing you can do to make any of this go away, because you aren't ill. In fact, the doctor says you're in perfect health and that your body is working just fine. He also says that in a few months you'll be back to normal.

You hope he's right. You also hope that your partner will be patient enough to hang in there with you, and not run off with someone who looks slimmer, or has more energy. Sure, they say they love you to bits, and you know deep down that they're telling the truth, but that still doesn't make you feel any better. Not totally anyway.

It's to be hoped that seeing the whole pregnancy thing from a woman's perspective will help *you* to understand where your partner is coming from when she's snappy, or tired, or weepy. The fact is, she really can't help those things. Her hormones are playing football inside her body, and they won't stop until the full-time whistle blows. So in the meantime, give her your support. Tell her you love her, often. Then back your words up with actions that help, assist and make her life as comfortable as possible.

Coping with your partner's mood swings

We have already seen how your partner's emotions are affected by the hormonal changes taking place in her body, but apart from giving you a very good reason to be more patient, that knowledge doesn't really help you to cope with them on a day-to-day basis. What you need are practical suggestions that you can actually use as and when the need arises. Here, then, are five simple strategies that you can employ to help both you and your partner cope effectively with mood swings.

Strategy 1: Don't always expect a logical explanation

If your partner is crying, it is perfectly natural to ask, 'What's wrong?' Unfortunately, during pregnancy there is often no logical explanation for the distress, and your partner will be as confused as you are about her state. The thing to do here is to offer love, support and reassurance. Tell your partner that you've read how this kind of thing is common, and most probably just her hormones tormenting her, then wrap your arms around her and tell her you love her. It's a very simple strategy, but it works.

Strategy 2: Deal with any logical explanation

Sometimes there will be a logical explanation for your partner's distress. For example, she may be worried about the additional expense that having a baby involves. Or she might be frightened about what giving birth will feel like.

In these situations, the best approach is to reassure your partner and focus on finding solutions to any practical problems that might be present. Worry and distress are often experienced when it appears that no solution to a problem exists, or when your partner doesn't have enough information to ease her fears, so by focusing on finding solutions in these areas, you will help your partner to feel more secure and positive.

Strategy 3: Don't withdraw unless requested

It seems to be a natural male instinct to pull away from situations that have a strong emotional content. Unfortunately, if you do this with your partner, she will probably conclude that you are rejecting her personally, and her state will only get worse. The best thing to do in most cases is therefore to draw closer to your partner and offer lots of gentle hugs, as well as verbal reassurances of your love.

The only exception to this is when your partner asks you to leave her alone for a while. When this happens, don't take her request as a rejection of you, but simply recognise the fact that she, like all of us, needs occasional time alone to think things through at her own pace.

Strategy 4: Be proactive

Your partner is pregnant, and what she probably wants most of all is to see that you are committed to being a great dad. If she feels that she has to bully you into making preparations for your new child, she may conclude that you aren't as keen on having the baby as she is, so aim to be proactive throughout the pregnancy. As you will see in a little while, there's a lot to do before your baby arrives, so take the initiative and start getting things done. When your partner sees that you are enthusiastic and proactive, she will feel a lot more secure and far less vulnerable than she might otherwise.

Strategy 5: Make time to talk

The final strategy is simply to talk. Make a point of sitting down with your partner each day and discussing things in a relaxed and positive way. Ask her how she's feeling, and if there's anything you can do to help make her feel more comfortable. This kind of concern is always appreciated, and if your partner knows that you are willing to talk about things openly, she is less likely to let her feelings bottle up to the point where they overwhelm her.

Sex during pregnancy

We live in a culture that separates motherhood from sexuality, and as soon as women cross the line from 'non-pregnant' to 'pregnant' it often seems as if they have also migrated from 'sexual beings' to 'non-sexual beings'. Men therefore get all sorts of mixed feelings about the issue of having sex during pregnancy. On the one hand they'd like to have sex with their partner just as much as they did before the pregnancy. But on the other hand, there's a baby in there somewhere, so won't sex hurt it? And even if it won't, will she think you're being an insensitive ape for even suggesting such a thing?

The good news is that women often have very similar hang-ups. Obviously, hormonal changes can put women off sex from time to time, but these changes can also have the reverse effect, and many have reported that being pregnant has actually made them feel even more sexual than before. But, like men, they often worry about whether it's safe to enjoy their increased libido, or whether they should keep quiet about it instead.

The bottom line is that if the pregnancy is progressing normally (meaning that there is no increased risk of miscarriage, etc.), there is no reason why you shouldn't both continue to enjoy a healthy sex life. If either of you is in any doubt whatsoever about this matter, simply have a quick word with your doctor for confirmation one way or the other.

Of course, the kind of sex you have during pregnancy might be different from the kind of sex you had beforehand. This is especially true in the third trimester, when having sex in the missionary position, for example, might not be as practical as it was before because of your partner's new body shape. It is therefore likely that you will want to be more creative, trying more appropriate positions or perhaps enjoying non-penetrative sexual activities.

Open communication is important here. Ask your partner what she would like, and make sure that she feels able to tell you if she is at all uncomfortable with having sex in a particular position. If she is, try something else. Finding out what works for you as a couple and what doesn't can often require a lot of experimenting, so have fun and enjoy the process.

Preparing for the birth of your child

Although it can often feel like pregnancy lasts forever, it doesn't, and you need to make sure that you're both physically and mentally prepared for a new baby in your home. This means planning ahead and equipping yourself to make the transition from pregnancy to labour to having a child in your home go as smoothly as possible.

Most importantly, your partner will need to make some important decisions concerning her birthing options. Although the majority of births take place in a maternity ward bed at a local hospital, other options, such as home births (giving birth at home) and water births (giving birth in a pool of water known as a 'birthing pool') are also available. She must also decide whether or not she would like to receive pain-relieving drugs during labour, or grit her teeth and take the drug-free route. All of these decisions can be made only once all relevant information has been gathered (such as the birthing options available in your specific area) and professional medical advice has been taken.

Since it's your partner who will have to go through the process of giving birth, your role here is to be a supporter, and not necessarily an influencer. You can share your views on the subject, of course, but remember that the final decision about this is not yours to make.

From your point of view, a major part of preparing for your first child is equipping the home. Your baby will need a cot, blankets, baby carriage, nappies, changing mat or table, bath, toys (a mobile or two in the first instance), clothes, feeding supplies (bottles and formula or nipple pads and possibly a breast pump if breast feeding), thermometer, car seat and a baby carrier. There are many other items that can also be obtained as 'optional extras', but the best idea is to focus on the essentials first and make sure that those are in place before shopping for other items.

If your child will be in a room of its own, you will need to spend time preparing this so that it is both comfortable and safe, with the emphasis on safety. To this end, always make a point of checking the safety certification of any product you buy, especially things like cots, mattresses, baby carriages and car seats. A good way of making more informed purchasing decisions is to buy a few baby magazines and read their reviews on the various products available.

From a practical point of view, it is usually a good idea to make a comprehensive list of things you will need to obtain and/or do, so that you can work your way through it and cross off each item as you go. This will prevent you from forgetting something, and ensures that you won't turn up to collect your baby from the hospital (or birthing pool) and suddenly remember that you haven't yet got an appropriate car seat. The list will also help you to estimate how much time all of the various preparations will take (decorating your child's room, for example) so that you can schedule the activities and get everything done.

One last thing here: Don't schedule everything as if your new baby will turn up exactly on time. The 40-week gestation period quoted by doctors is just an average. Babies are often a couple of weeks early or a couple of weeks late. This isn't surprising when you consider that they don't have a copy of the doctor's estimated date of delivery. So, always plan to get things done at least a week or two before your partner's due date.

SUMMARY OF CHAPTER 2

- Being a great dad begins as soon as your partner is confirmed pregnant.

- For purposes of discussion, pregnancy is divided into three stages, called trimesters.

- Pregnancy is no picnic for your partner. She will, at times, suffer from nausea, tiredness, stress and a variety of other side-effects. So be supportive!

- Looking at things from your partner's point of view will enable you to be more compassionate and patient.

- You can cope with your partner's mood swings by employing five simple strategies:
    - Strategy 1: Don't always expect a logical explanation.
    - Strategy 2: Deal with any logical explanation.
    - Strategy 3: Don't withdraw unless requested.
    - Strategy 4: Be proactive.
    - Strategy 5: Make time to talk.

- Sex during a normal pregnancy is usually perfectly safe, but you may need to be more creative about positions. Ask your partner for her ideas on comfortable sex.

- You need to prepare for the birth of your child in advance. Make a list of all the things you need to obtain and/or do, then work through the list in a logical manner.

CHAPTER 3

Your D-Day Mission

By the time your partner enters the ninth month of pregnancy, you might both be feeling as if the gestation of your child is something that will never end. Fortunately, it will, and – like in all the best movies – it will end in style, with the delivery of your new child. On D-Day there will be screaming, shouting, some scenes which may affect those of a squeamish or nervous disposition, and perhaps some panic thrown in for good measure. And that, my friends, is why you need to prepare yourself for what I like to refer to as your D-Day Mission.

Your mission on D-Day itself is to support your partner as she gives birth. It sounds fairly simple, doesn't it? But there's more to it than just showing up and wiping a cool flannel across your partner's forehead once every fifteen minutes – a lot more. We'll look at the detailed ins and outs of labour (let's be honest, they're mostly outs) a little later, but first let us pause to discuss a few practical arrangements which need to be made.

Booking time off work

Your first practical task is to book time off work with your employer so that you can be present at the birth and spend the following few days supporting your partner and taking care of your new child. The biggest problem here is in not knowing when D-Day will arrive. It has been said that only five per cent of pregnant women actually give birth on their estimated date. The majority of the remaining ninety-five per cent will give birth up to a fortnight before or a fortnight after their estimated date.

This lack of certainty about exactly when your baby will be

delivered into the world used to make planning time off work quite difficult. However, fairly recent legislation has given fathers an automatic right to paternity leave as long as you meet certain qualifications published by the Department of Trade and Industry. Whilst it isn't usually necessary to study the law in detail on this topic, it is important that you understand what you are entitled to as a new father. For this reason, I will now provide the main details for you to take a look at. All italicised statements in this section are © Crown copyright.

An employee must satisfy the following conditions in order to qualify for paternity leave. He must

- *have or expect to have responsibility for the child's upbringing*

- *be the biological father of the child or the mother's husband or partner*

- *have worked continuously for his employer for 26 weeks ending with the fifteenth week before the baby is due.*

Eligible employees can choose to take either one week or two consecutive weeks' paternity leave (not odd days). They can choose to start their leave

- *from the date of the child's birth (whether this is earlier or later than expected); or*

- *from a chosen number of days or weeks after the date of the child's birth (whether this is earlier or later than expected); or*

- *from a chosen date later than the first day of the week in which the baby is expected to be born.*

Leave can start on any day of the week on or following the child's birth but must be completed

- *within 56 days of the actual date of birth of the child; or*

- *if the child is born early, within the period from the actual date of birth up to 56 days after the first day of the expected week of birth.*

Only one period of leave is available to employees irrespective of whether more than one child is born as the result of the same pregnancy.

During their paternity leave, most employees are entitled to Statutory Paternity Pay (SPP) from their employer. SPP is paid by employers for either one or two consecutive weeks as the employee has chosen. The rate of SPP is the same as the standard rate of Statutory Maternity Pay.

Employees who have average weekly earnings below the lower earnings limit for National Insurance purposes do not qualify for SPP. Employees who do not qualify for SPP, or who are normally low-paid, may be able to get Income Support while on paternity leave. Additional financial support may be available through Housing Benefit, Council Tax Benefit, Tax Credits or a Sure Start Maternity Grant. Further information is available from your local Jobcentre Plus office or Social Security office.

An employee must inform the employer of his intention to take paternity leave by the end of the fifteenth week before the baby is expected, unless this is not reasonably practicable. He must tell the employer:

- *the week the baby is due*

- *whether he wishes to take one or two weeks' leave*

- *when he wants the leave to start.*

The employee can change his mind about the date on which he wants the leave to start provided he tells the employer at least 28 days in advance (unless this is not reasonably practicable). The employee must tell the employer the date he expects any payments of SPP to start at least 28 days in advance, unless this is not reasonably practicable.

The employee must give the employer a completed self-certificate as evidence of entitlement to SPP. A model self-certificate for employers and employees to use is available in Working Fathers: Rights to Leave and Pay (PL517). *Employers can also request a completed self-certificate as evidence of entitlement to paternity leave. The self-certificate must include a declaration that the employee meets certain eligibility conditions and provide the information specified above as part of the notice requirements.*

By providing a completed self-certificate, an employee will be able to satisfy both the notice and evidence conditions for paternity leave and pay. Employers will not be expected to carry out any further checks.

Employees are entitled to the benefit of their normal terms and conditions of employment – except for terms relating to wages or salary (unless their contract of employment provides otherwise) – throughout their paternity leave. However, most employees will be entitled to SPP for this period. If the employee has a contractual right to paternity leave as well as the statutory right, he may take advantage of whichever is the more favourable. Any paternity pay to which he has a contractual right reduces the amount of SPP to which he is entitled.

Employees are protected from suffering unfair treatment or dismissal for taking, or seeking to take, paternity leave. Employees who believe they have been treated unfairly can complain to an employment tribunal. Employees are entitled to return to the same job following paternity leave.

Now that these rights and entitlements have been given to fathers, booking time off work shouldn't pose too much of a problem. In most cases, it's simply a matter of discussing your situation with your employer and setting the necessary wheels in motion.

The overnight bag

Your partner will need an overnight bag which is ready to pick up and go a couple of weeks before her estimated date of delivery. This bag should contain all that she needs to spend a night in hospital (a toothbrush, nightdress, etc.). Your partner will probably want to prepare it herself, but offering to help with the task is a nice gesture and will reassure her that you are planning ahead so that everything runs as smoothly as possible.

A communication and procedure agreement

Unless you happen to work from home or have unlimited leave from your job, you probably won't be able to guarantee that you will be with your partner when she goes into labour. This means that it's necessary to establish a way for your partner to get in touch with you quickly as soon as she needs to. Most people opt to use a mobile telephone or pager, as these can be carried around discreetly as you go about your usual business, but if there is another method of communication you prefer then feel free to use it. Just make sure that your partner knows exactly how to reach you when the time comes.

You also need to discuss with your partner what to do when she goes into labour. If you work nearby then it shouldn't be a problem for you to dash home and collect your wife (and her overnight bag) yourself. However, if you don't work close to home, you need to come up with a Plan B, such as phoning an agreeable friend or neighbour, for example.

All of this pre-planning might sound a little over the top, but it really isn't. The fact is that going into labour can be a scary experience – especially for a woman who hasn't given birth before – and discussing various scenarios with her beforehand (such as what she would do if she went into labour whilst shopping) will help her to keep relatively calm when the time actually comes.

Labour and childbirth

Like pregnancy itself, the labour process is often divided into three stages to make it more easily discussed. The *first stage of labour* begins with regular contractions. Contractions, which are experienced as cramp-like pains in the lower back and lower abdomen, serve to bring the baby into position so that the mother can later give birth. Initially, the contractions may be quite mild with relatively long gaps between each one, but as this first stage of labour continues they become more intense and more frequent. This stage of labour often lasts several hours and ends when the cervix is fully dilated to ten centimetres.

In the *second stage of labour* – which is the one most people think of when they discuss 'being in labour' in general conversation – contractions become even more intense, last longer and are more frequent (every couple of minutes or so). Over a few hours, the baby is pushed down the birth canal, the top of the head becomes visible to external observers (this is known as 'crowning'), and the baby is born shortly afterwards.

Incidentally, don't expect your child to look particularly clean when he or she emerges. Most newborn babies have a purple colour, and will look quite sticky and messy. This is all perfectly normal, considering where they've been living for the past nine months – but if you aren't prepared for it, the sight can be a little shocking.

The *third stage of labour* is the shortest of the three and follows the birth of the baby. Another series of contractions will be experienced by your partner in order to deliver the placenta. Often, your baby will have been taken by the midwife to be quickly cleaned, weighed and checked over for any problems. The baby will then generally be handed to the mother or yourself, depending on whether or not your partner has already expelled the placenta.

You should bear in mind that all of this is textbook stuff, and that real life sometimes deviates from the routine. Some babies need to be delivered by caesarean section in order to safeguard the health of the mother, baby or both. Sometimes a woman will tear as she gives birth. This can result in quite a lot of bleeding, and stitches may be required after the third stage of labour. Be prepared for such surprises, and be prepared for quite a messy sight. But most of all, have faith in the medical experts who will be taking care of your partner. They have seen everything possible, and they know how to deal with situations effectively, so if they decide they need to take action of some sort, step out of the way and let them get on with doing their job.

Coping with false alarms ... and the real thing

Often a woman will experience contractions and believe that she is going into labour, then get to the hospital and discover that it was a false alarm. This can be very frustrating, especially for your partner, who will naturally have been gearing herself up psychologically to deal with the full three-stage process just outlined, and looking forward to seeing her new baby for the very first time. It is not uncommon for a woman to feel a little embarrassed for having being 'taken in' by a false alarm, but the truth is that telling the difference between a series of more intense Braxton Hicks contractions and the contractions which mark the onset of labour can be extremely difficult – especially if the woman has not given birth previously.

In these 'false alarm' situations, be patient, supportive and understanding. Reassure your partner that she's perfectly sane and normal, that false alarms are common, and that the real thing will take place before much longer.

When the real thing does occur, it is important to try to keep calm and be patient. As you have seen, labour can take many hours from beginning to end, so being impatient or in a hurry will only lead to unnecessary frustration.

Understanding what she's going through – II

For obvious biological reasons, it's impossible for a man to be able to imagine having a vagina. So, for the purposes of this section, we'll have to use a bit of 'artistic licence' and do the best we can with the equipment we have available:

Your body has been growing for nine long, tiring months. Your belly, which used to be toned and trim, is now distended so far that you can't see your feet when standing. Your lower back aches and your ankles are swollen from carrying the extra weight. You feel a cramp in your lower abdomen. It lasts about fifteen seconds, then fades. Ten minutes later, there's another one. Then another. They come regularly, first at ten-minute intervals, then more often. By the time they are coming once every five minutes, each one lasts for around thirty seconds and you know you're going into labour.

The thought is both soothing and frightening. On the one hand, it means you won't have to carry around all of this excess weight for much longer. But on the other hand, it also means that you'll have to push something slightly larger than a regulation rugby ball out of your vagina, and that doesn't sound so good right now.

As your 'labour' progresses, the cramps come more frequently and are increasingly painful. Each one brings the rugby ball closer to where the sun never shines, and you realise that no matter how much worse it gets, there's no going back. Your body will have to stretch to accommodate the 'birth' or it will tear itself trying.

I'll leave the rest to your imagination, as I think you should be getting a rough idea right now of what your partner will have to go through. But just remember – this is only a mind game as far as you are concerned. Your partner isn't reading some creative simulation in a book, she's doing this stuff for real, so remember that and act accordingly.

Your D-Day action plan

When she's in labour, your partner will feel fairly isolated. Yes, she'll be surrounded by medical experts and have you on hand, but she'll be the only one who has to experience the pain, fear and exhaustion of the occasion first-hand. Whilst there's no way you can relieve your partner of this, there are some things that you can do throughout her labour to try to make the process just a tad more comfortable.

- *Offer her drinks.* Giving birth is thirsty work, and your partner will probably want to have some fluid on hand at all times. Be there to give her water (or whatever drink she has planned on) as and when she needs it.

- *Have a cool facecloth ready for her.* Your partner will get very hot and sweaty during labour (it's extremely hard work, after all) and mopping her brow every now and again will be appreciated.

- *Hold her hand.* Many women like to hold the hand of their partner during especially painful phases, so be there for her.

● *Talk to her.* Tell her you love her. Tell her she's doing great. Encourage her to relax when the midwife wants her to relax. Encourage her to push when the midwife wants her to push. All of this verbal support will be appreciated.

These are all things that you can do to be supportive, but don't be surprised if – at some point during the proceedings – your partner begins to express things other than appreciation. The fact is that her brain will go into 'survival mode' in order to cope with the incredible pain she's experiencing, and this can lead to a kind of Jekyll and Hyde transformation you really will have to witness to believe.

No matter what kind of woman your partner is, you can expect to be surprised. When you try to comfort her verbally, she may tell you to shut your mouth and keep quiet. When you try to mop her brow, she may tell you to get away from her. When you go to hold her hand, she may dig her nails in so far that you bleed. She may tell you that the pain she is experiencing is all your fault, since you were the one who made her pregnant. She may tell you that she hates you. She may swear at you like a trooper, using expletives with such vicious dexterity that you'll start believing in demonic possession.

It's important to understand that what your partner says or does during labour needs to be taken in context. As far as her brain is concerned, she's fighting for survival in there, so let all negative comments come at you and then let them go. Don't start arguing or denying anything, but just agree with whatever she says. If she says that you're a wimp, a control freak or, paradoxically, both a wimp and a control freak, just accept the comments and let her get on with the job at hand.

The labour process, as you should realise by now, will be a fairly intense experience for both of you. The good news is that once the pain and the exhaustion and the stress and the expletives have all had a chance to calm down, you'll be left with the one thing that makes it all worthwhile – your newborn baby.

SUMMARY OF CHAPTER 3

- Your mission on D-Day is to support your partner as she gives birth.
- You need to prepare for the event in advance.
- False alarms are common. If your partner has a false alarm, be supportive and understanding.
- For purposes of discussion, labour is divided into three stages. The whole process can take many hours, so be patient and allow things to run their course.
- You should be as helpful as you can be during the labour process, but don't be surprised if your partner seems to undergo a Jekyll and Hyde transformation. Instead, roll with the punches and remember that it's all perfectly normal.
- The reward which makes everything worthwhile is the new baby you share at the end of the experience. Enjoy the moment – your lives are now going to be a great deal richer.

CHAPTER 4

The First Two Weeks

Can you remember when you went to a particular school for the very first time and spent a whole week just getting used to the new layout, new teachers and new routines? Or when you started a new job and spent a couple of days adjusting to the reality of the work involved, rather than the job description? This kind of reality check happens to new dads too. No matter how much you've prepared yourself psychologically, no matter how much parenting theory you have under your belt, the first two weeks of actually being a father can come as quite a shock. This is not because you don't know what to expect, but simply because you have to learn how to deal with a myriad of things in real time. In this chapter we'll look at what the first two weeks usually involve, and suggest ways of not only coping with, but actually enjoying, the demanding learning curve.

Sustenance

Sleeping

One of the first things you will notice is that babies sleep a lot more than you might have expected. It is normal for newborns to sleep as much as sixteen hours a day in the beginning, so it's important to make sure that good sleeping arrangements are in place from the outset.

Try to make sure that the room your child is sleeping in (be it the bedroom at night or the lounge during the day) is free from draughts and has a fairly consistent average temperature. The medical staff at the hospital will have demonstrated how to wrap your child safely in a blanket, so keep using that method when you get home. Don't use pillows in the sleeping area, or put your baby on a pillow on your own bed, as the infant is not yet able to lift his or her head and could therefore suffocate. Get into the habit of putting your baby in its own crib to sleep rather than take any unnecessary risks.

Having said that babies can sleep for up to sixteen hours a day, this isn't all at once. Although each baby is an individual, they generally sleep in short sessions of two or three hours. This means that, despite the quantity of sleep they have, getting a baby to sleep through the night is virtually impossible for at least the first few months. Plan on feeding and changing your baby several times a night rather than getting frustrated by unrealistic expectations. Respond to your baby quickly and the chances are that, once he has been fed, changed or cuddled for a while, he will be perfectly happy to go back to sleep. But if you allow your baby to cry for longer than a minute or two before responding, he will get himself so worked up that the chances of him going back to sleep decline rapidly.

It is important to understand that this sporadic sleeping pattern can make both you and your partner a little more tired and irritable during the day. Fortunately, this doesn't last long, as human beings adjust relatively quickly to their circumstances and eventually you will find it quite easy to sleep in several shorter bursts rather than in one long eight-hour session. But until then, be patient with each other and try to grab some rest as and when you can. In other words, if your baby decides to sleep for a couple of hours on a Saturday morning after a particularly fragmented night, suggest that both you and your partner do the same.

Babies tend to settle into a more 'civilised' sleeping pattern after a few months, and at this time can often sleep for five or six hours in a single stretch. When this happens, enjoy it. By then a straight six hours will feel like the best lie-in you've ever had.

Feeding ...

Babies have incredibly small stomachs, and because they are on a liquid diet for the first few months of life they get hungry on a regular basis. You should therefore expect to feed your baby every two to six hours, day and night.

There are two main choices when it comes to feeding a newborn and these are to breast-feed or use an infant formula. In most circumstances, breast-feeding is the ideal choice because it not only provides all the nutrition your baby needs, but is also convenient (in terms of preparation, if not presentation) and helps the mother and child bond incredibly effectively. For those who are unable or unwilling to breast-feed, infant formula is the alternative. This involves a lot more preparation (sterilisation of bottles, mixing and warming of formula, etc.) but does offer slightly more convenience when it comes to feeding in public.

It is important to burp a baby after feeding so that gas doesn't build up in the stomach and cause discomfort. It is also a good idea to have a towel or cloth handy when you do this, because it is quite common for some liquid to come up with the gas, and in my experience it is more common when you are least prepared for it to happen.

... and dirty nappies

Between taking naps and feeding, your baby will still find time to fill a surprisingly large number of nappies. But possibly more surprising are the contents – at least for the first few days. Bowel movements initially result in the expulsion of something called meconium. This is a thick, sticky and very dark green – almost black – substance at first, but the colour lightens gradually, through lighter green and then to yellow or beige. Granted, these aren't the kind of details you'd like to share with a friend over dinner, but it's important to know what to expect so that you don't panic when meconium happens.

One skill that you will have to learn quickly is how to change nappies. Fortunately this isn't technically difficult, and perhaps the hardest part is getting accustomed to the smell.

First, get everything you need in one place: nappy, cotton wool and water (or baby wipes), dry wipes, and so on. French chefs call this kind of advanced preparation *mise en place,* and one of the main advantages is that it's quicker and cleaner to prepare everything beforehand than it is to muddle through as you go along.

Next, place a paper towel on a changing mat or changing table and place the baby on top of that (so that the towel can contain any spillage).

Remove the nappy, hold your breath and clean up as necessary. If you have a baby boy be aware that he does have a penis and even now his aim will be remarkably well developed – especially when you are changing him. Goggles are optional.

To fit the fresh nappy, hold the ankles of your baby and raise her or him up slightly so that you can slide the backside of the nappy under the backside of the baby. Then bring the front of the nappy up between the legs and around the belly, being careful to avoid irritating the umbilical cord region.

Now all you have to do, apart from putting the baby in a safe place and cleaning up, is hope that your baby will wait an hour or two before demanding that you repeat the exercise all over again.

What you can expect to experience emotionally

The three big 'practical' issues of sleeping, feeding and dirty nappies will demand a lot of your time during the first two weeks, but there are emotional issues which also need to be discussed. Becoming a father may take nine months biologically speaking, but the reality of going from not having a baby to having a baby often takes less than twenty-four hours. This can leave you feeling a little shell-shocked, and it would not be at all uncommon for you to experience feelings of inadequacy. Here's why:

Having a new baby can make you feel that you aren't yet mature enough to cope. This feeling stems from the mistaken belief that some men are 'ready' for fatherhood and others – always including yourself – are not. The fact is that all men, if they are honest about it, feel at least a twinge of doubt about whether or not they are mature enough to have another human being depending on them to the extent that a baby does. The good news is that if you simply accept the responsibility and work with it (rather than run away from it) you will mature into your new role automatically.

Having a new baby can make you feel that you aren't successful enough. As we've already said, children are expensive, and the older they get, the more expensive they tend to become. If you don't feel confident in your ability to provide for your new baby, you aren't likely to feel that great – at least initially. To deal with this emotion, just remember that – so far – you might not have had a very good reason to focus on achieving financial success, and that having a new baby might provide the impetus you need to make more progress in this area of your life.

Having a new baby can make you feel like a party pooper. Your partner, having carried the baby for nine months, is naturally going to focus a lot of attention on her new child, and this means that you probably won't get the level of attention that you used to enjoy before the birth. Rather than feel down about this, focus on giving your child and partner more attention and begin to see yourself more as a giver than a taker. As time passes, sharing love with each other as a family will become the most natural thing on earth for you, and you will probably find that your one-on-one relationship with your partner actually improves rather than deteriorates.

Having a new baby can make you feel overwhelmed and frustrated. This happens when you realise just how much work is involved in caring for a newborn, and you start thinking about how little time you have to get everything done. Once again, this is a temporary feeling, and within a few weeks you will be handling everything as if you'd been doing it for years, so remind yourself of this whenever the going gets tough.

So much for your emotional responses, but what about the emotions of your partner? Well, as you might expect, these can be even more pronounced. Just as her hormonal fluctuations affected her mood in the early weeks of pregnancy, so they will do so in the early weeks of motherhood. All of the emotions that you can experience apply equally for women, but in addition, post-natal depression is a fairly common experience. Because of this, don't get overly worried if your partner seems a little quieter than usual for a few days. She has a lot of thinking of her own to do, and – like you – will need some time to adjust to the new situation.

You can support your partner by helping her take physical

care of the baby as much as possible and by helping out with household chores. This will give her more time and space to adjust emotionally. You should also continue your habit of encouraging open communication and offering lots of comforting hugs and spoken words of appreciation. This 'depressed' state of mind generally only lasts a short while, so if it continues for more than a week it may be worth encouraging your partner to visit her doctor for additional support.

Understanding what she's going through – III

First you got large, heavy and tired. Then you went through the most frightening and painful experience of your life, which was – paradoxically – one of the most joyous experiences of your life at the same time. At this point you expected to feel relieved, relaxed and happy. And of course you are, at times. But at other times you are hit by waves of less joyous emotions and feel overwhelmed, alone, frightened and insecure.

Last week you were okay. You had to take care of yourself and you were secure in the knowledge that your partner could take care of himself as well. But now you have a tiny human being who is one hundred per cent reliant on you, twenty-four hours a day, seven days a week, and this takes some getting used to.

From now on, you realise that you can never again think only of your own well-being. Every decision that you make has to take into consideration the well-being of this tiny, helpless human being. Should you ever withdraw your support, this delicate human being will die. You are suddenly aware of the enormous responsibility resting on your shoulders, and at times it just feels like too much. In fact at times you wonder if you're really cut out to be a parent at all. It just doesn't feel at all natural to you right now ... and you have no idea of whether things will get better with time (as everyone tells you they will) or whether you will feel like this permanently.

You should note that not every woman who gives birth experiences this kind of emotional response, or to this degree. However, by being aware of how it is possible for a woman to feel, you will be better equipped to relate to your partner more sympathetically, rather than expect her to be jumping with joy immediately.

Setting up a support system and protecting family time

Because having your first baby can be tiring, stressful and emotionally demanding, it is a good idea to set up a support system. All new parents get a certain amount of support from health visitors and so on, but if you can also enlist the help of a few carefully selected friends and relatives, so much the better.

What kind of support should you be looking for? The answer is simple – whatever you need in your personal circumstances. You may want someone to help with shopping, or to provide advice from time to time. Or it could be that you'd simply like someone to drop by every couple of days for a coffee and a chat so that you and your partner don't lose touch with the outside world.

There is no real need to be formal about setting up a support system, but you do need to give it some conscious thought. Discuss the idea with your partner and identify what kind of support you need. Then go from there and enlist the aid of friends and family members who are willing and able to provide the additional help required.

As well as setting up a support system, you will also need to protect your time as a family by controlling exactly who visits on any given day. Having a baby is obviously a cause for celebration, but some people seem to think that you'll be wanting to accept visitors at all hours and they often don't realise that you also need time to yourselves. As a great dad, it is your responsibility to ensure that your child and partner aren't so swamped with visitors that they don't have time to relax.

The best way to do this is to ask people to phone ahead before visiting to arrange a suitable time. By taking this approach you can ensure that you don't get too many people visiting on any given day, and thereby protect a certain amount of time so that you can enjoy being alone with your partner and baby.

The first two weeks of life with your new baby can often feel like you are on an emotional rollercoaster. On some days it will be stressful, frustrating, busy and tiring. Yet on other days you will feel extremely fulfilled and happy. Overall, it will be an experience you will never forget, so be sure to pause every now and again to enjoy it as it unfolds.

SUMMARY OF CHAPTER 4

- The first two weeks of parenthood can be viewed as a period of adjustment to your new circumstances and responsibilities.
- It is normal for newborn babies to sleep for up to sixteen hours each day.
- You should expect to feed your baby every two to six hours, day and night.
- The first few bowel movements of a newborn consist of a dark green (almost black) substance known as meconium. This is perfectly normal.
- It is also normal for both you and your partner to experience a wide range of emotions as you adjust to your new baby.
- Set up a support system to help you and your partner in the difficult early days. At the same time, protect your family time by asking visitors to phone in advance.
- The first two weeks of fatherhood will be an experience you will never forget, so be sure to pause every now and again to enjoy it as it unfolds.

CHAPTER 5

Your Role as a Great Dad

Being a great dad is not like being a great craftsman. A great craftsman can master one particular set of skills and then continue using those same skills day in and day out, year after year, with no loss of effectiveness. A great dad can't do this. Your role as a great dad will have to change as your children grow. If it doesn't, you won't be as great as you could be. Of course, some things – such as giving love unconditionally and leading by example – can and should remain constant no matter how old your child is. But even here, your approach must change if you want to be consistently successful in the years ahead.

For example, when you are the father of a toddler, you will take a particular approach to matters such as discipline and education. This will work well in the context of raising a toddler, but if you were to try to employ the same approach to raising a ten-year-old, or a teenager, you simply won't be very effective. Not because the approach itself is invalid, but simply because it isn't the most suitable one to use with an older child.

Because being a great dad over the long term requires that you learn to adapt your approach as your child grows and matures, some of the chapters from this point on will look at a specific aspect of fatherhood over four time frames.

Ages 0 to 5

The first five years of life are ones in which your child makes dramatic progress, not just physically, but also intellectually, emotionally and socially. The leap from being a newborn who is totally dependent on others for virtually everything, to becoming a much more independent five-year-old who can feed and clean himself or herself, as well as walk, talk and play games, is a truly remarkable one. It's also a crucial one for you as a great dad.

Throughout this phase of life, your child will learn chiefly by interacting with, and following the example of, adults. If a child sees his father picking his nose in front of the television on a daily basis, he will assume that this is a good 'grown up' habit to have, and will therefore start doing it himself. Of course, the good news is that this tendency to follow adult example works equally well with positive habits. If a child sees his father exercise each day and enjoy eating fruits and vegetables, he will start adopting these habits just as easily. Always remember that, when it comes down to the bottom line, what you do speaks far louder than what you say.

Of course, what you say still counts for a great deal. One of the major breakthroughs for a child in this phase is learning to communicate. The language a child is exposed to in these crucial years will become part of his or her habitual vocabulary. This means that if you don't want your child to swear like a trooper, you're going to have to make sure you don't unwittingly teach this through your own vocabulary. And if you want the child to be polite and get into the habit of saying please and thank you, you will need to ensure that you too do this whenever it's appropriate.

You also need to be aware that these are the years in which a child begins to form an identity. Since you are a significant role model in your child's life, he or she will look to you when trying to understand being a human being. This means that if you routinely call your boy stupid or lazy or naughty then he will begin to see himself in this way, and act appropriately. You should therefore resolve to start helping your child to develop a positive and empowering self-image by praising every success, using encouraging words and phrases.

In these first five years, it is perfectly normal for children to test boundaries in order to learn the difference between what is acceptable behaviour and what is unacceptable behaviour. It is also perfectly normal for the child to deliberately disobey as he or she begins to try to assert their will on the world. Remember that these phases don't last forever and are just a part of the natural learning process. However, if you have to criticise something, criticise the behaviour rather than your child. Saying that 'throwing toys at the TV is naughty' is a lot more accurate than saying 'you are a naughty boy'. The former phrase criticises the behaviour, but the latter phrase criticises your child and could have a negative effect on his or her developing self-image. We will look at this important subject a little more when we examine psychological and emotional health in Chapter 8.

The bottom line here is that your role as a great dad for this first phase of life should be to focus on teaching by example. Understand that your daily actions have a very large impact on your child and will form the basis for future habits and actions. Don't just tell your child what ought to be done, but show this repeatedly by doing the same yourself.

Ages 6 to 10

From the ages of six to ten, children become even more independent. They start developing their own taste in clothes, choosing their own friends and making their own distinctions about the world they live in. Whereas a four- or five-year-old might have blindly believed every word you said, children between the ages of six and ten will start questioning things and forming their own opinions – which is probably why Santa Claus tends to lose most of his appeal around about now.

To be a great dad in this phase of your child's life, you need to continue to focus on setting a good example, but increasingly you will also need to explain your motivations for asking that things be done in a certain way. Saying 'Don't play ball indoors' will commonly result in a simple response: 'Why?' This isn't because your child is trying to be difficult, but because he or she genuinely wants to know why ball games are not suitable indoors. Unfortunately, if you come back with 'Because I said so, that's why!' then you're missing a great opportunity to teach your child about cause and effect. It would be better to explain that playing ball indoors could lead to something being smashed, or to someone getting hurt. Very often, when children understand the reason for doing something or not doing something, they begin to comply with such requests without argument. You may need to explain the same cause and effect relationship several times before they really get it, but if you choose to explain it rather than demand compliance just because you've said so, you will have plenty of opportunities to teach your child about cause, effect and the importance of taking personal responsibility.

It is during this phase of life that most kids start making and breaking relationships with friends. They begin to see themselves not only as individuals, but as members of society. They begin to categorise their peers as members of separate groups – as friends, enemies and floating voters – and they begin adjusting their interactions with others on the basis of these internal distinctions. They begin to have their first experiences of peer pressure (which is discussed in Chapter 9) and learn quickly about both acceptance and rejection, and about what is 'cool' and what is 'not cool'.

Facing such issues as these can be challenging at times, so you will need to be particularly supportive and help your child to deal with them effectively. What you need to instil in your child now – if it isn't already – is the fact that you are on the same side and that he or she can come to you for help and support whenever it is needed, on problems both big and small. If your child is happy to come to you for help with small problems now, he or she is likely to come to you for help in the future, when the problems faced could potentially be a lot bigger.

Ages 11 to 15

There are two words which make many parents want to shrivel up and hide in a corner: puberty and adolescence. The first naturally leads to the second, and you will have to deal with both issues in this third phase of your child's life. If this notion terrifies you, relax. It's something that all parents have to go through, and the reality is that it's just as potentially bewildering to your child as it is to you.

From a purely physiological perspective, your child will go through many changes, and you will need to be there to help educate them about what is happening and to give them support through the whole process. But you will also need to change your approach from an emotional perspective too.

This phase is where your child makes the gradual transition from being a fairly dependent human being to one who is, by age fifteen, capable of making most of his or her own decisions. The problem is that your son or daughter isn't quite there yet – not quite physically or emotionally mature enough to live independently, but often feeling otherwise.

If you continue to treat a child in this phase of life as you would a ten-year-old, you'll be rewarded with conflict, and lots of it. At the same time, if you give your child free rein then immaturity in certain areas could lead to trouble.

So what's the solution?

The solution – and the way to be a great dad – is to recognise this phase as the one in which you need to give your child more space. The older children get, the more room they need to feel independent rather than stifled. By increasing the amount of freedom and responsibility you give your child gradually, you can help to make the transition from puberty to young adulthood one that is as smooth and comfortable as possible.

Ages 16 to 20

This fourth and final phase is the one in which your child becomes an adult in his or her own right. Your child will now have to make some very tough decisions about where to go in life and how to get there. Your role as a great dad here is as a supporter and advisor. By this stage you will have given your child the freedom to make independent decisions, but you still need to be available if and when your child needs help with those decisions. The fact is that he or she doesn't yet have much life experience to draw upon when faced with difficult choices, so will often look to you for your input.

Being a great dad to a young adult means being willing to give advice, but not insisting that your advice be taken. This is one of the most difficult aspects of fatherhood to deal with, because it's now that you realise you are no longer indispensable as far as your child is concerned. Yes, the child still loves you as much as many years ago, but doesn't need you as much as back then.

By the time this phase is over (give or take a year), your child will be totally independent and have started forging a life of his or her own. Of course, a child is for life, and not just for the first twenty years – so in Chapter 16 we will look at Being a Great Dad to an Adult.

As you have seen, your role as a great dad must change in many different ways as your child grows from newborn to adulthood, so we will next look at the most important aspects of being a great dad and examine how the approach you take in each area needs to be adjusted as your child matures.

SUMMARY OF CHAPTER 5

- Although there are some things – such as giving love unconditionally and leading by example – that can and should remain constants no matter how old your child is, your role as a great dad will have to change as your children grow.

- Between ages 0 and 5, your role as a great dad should be to focus on teaching by example. Understand that your daily actions have a very large impact on your child and will form the basis for his or her own habits and actions. Don't only tell your child what he or she should do, but demonstrate repeatedly by doing the same yourself.

- Between ages 6 and 10, you need to continue to focus on setting a good example, but increasingly you will also need to explain your motivations for asking for things to be done in a certain way. You also need to instil in your child the fact that you are on the same side and that he or she can come to you for help and support on all problems.

- As your child goes through puberty and adolescence, you will need to be there to help educate about what is happening and provide support through the whole process. You also need to increase the amount of freedom and responsibility you give your child gradually, to make the transition from puberty to young adulthood one that is as smooth and comfortable as possible.

- Between ages 16 and 20, your role as a great dad is primarily as a supporter and advisor. By this stage, you will have given your child the freedom to make independent decisions, but you still need to be available if and when your child needs help with those decisions.

CHAPTER 6

Making Time for Fatherhood

From a kid's point of view

I know my dad loves me. He tells me all the time. And he's always giving me stuff. Last week it was a new computer game. The week before it was a CD by my favourite band. But sometimes I just wish he'd spend more time with me. I know he's busy, and he's always telling me how hard he has to work to pay the bills, so I try not to make a fuss about it. But, you know, I'd rather go without the computer games and CDs so he doesn't have to work so hard to pay for them. Maybe then he'd be able to give me what I really want ... just an hour or two in the evenings to play together, or a Saturday afternoon just having a laugh at the park.

Making time

There are two schools of thought regarding the kind of time children need in order to flourish. Some people argue that children need time in quantity, and that they need plenty of extended periods with their fathers to feel loved and secure. To these people, what you do during your time together is not deemed as important as the amount of time spent together. Others say that quantity is largely irrelevant, and that what children really want is quality time, where the father is devoting the whole of the time he spends with his children playing games, communicating and consciously making their time together as productive as possible.

I think the common sense approach lies somewhere between these two extremes. Yes, children do need to spend quality time with you so that they really feel connected, valued and loved. But they also need to be able to relax with you, rather than anxiously watching the clock just because they know you've only got a half-hour slot to devote to them. So quality and quantity are both equally important.

Having said that being a great dad takes time, where do we find the time required? This is a question that many fathers struggle with on a daily basis, but the answer is actually rather simple. Great dads don't bother trying to *find* the time to be with their kids. Instead, they *make* time to be with their kids.

No matter who we are, we all have exactly the same number of hours each day, the same number of days each week and the same number of weeks each year. How we spend those hours, days and weeks is very much up to us. Although we often complain that we have to do this or we have to do that, the truth is that nobody has to do anything they don't want to. We all have the power to choose how we spend our time based on our priorities.

Our priorities are the things that we consider to be extremely important to us. For most men, working for a living is a high priority because it enables us to provide for ourselves and our families. Hobbies, on the other hand, tend to be much lower on our list of priorities. So when it comes to deciding how we will spend our time, we naturally invest more in our work than we do in our hobbies, because that's the way we've prioritised things.

Unfortunately, most people never pause to consciously establish their personal list of priorities or deliberately plan how they will spend the time that they have available. This usually means that they waste a great deal of their time without even realising it.

For example, many men who have working for a living as their unconscious number one priority will turn up for work each morning, put in the required number of hours and then go home. The rest of the day will be spent doing a little of this and a little of that, with no real sense of purpose or focus. In brief, they end up majoring in minor things and spending quite a bit of their 'free' time on activities that aren't really important in the larger scheme of things – activities like watching TV, going to the pub and snoozing on the sofa.

Great dads don't do this. Instead, they choose to organise and live their lives in a more deliberate and conscious way so that they have all the time they need to be with their kids, and they do this by taking three simple steps:

- They consciously organise their list of priorities based on their personal needs and values.

- They divide the time they have available according to this list and schedule activities just as they would schedule important business meetings or medical appointments.

- They live to their schedule, thereby ensuring that their plan becomes a reality.

All of this may sound a little formal, but in practice it really isn't – it's just sensible organisation – and when you get used to the process it quickly becomes second nature. Let's go through each step in turn so that you can learn exactly how to manage your own time using this proven Great Dad system.

Three steps

Step 1: Consciously organise your priorities

Take a pad and pencil and sit down somewhere quiet for fifteen minutes or so. During this time, list the things that are really important to you in life, such as your relationship with your partner, your health, your children and your work. Then list other things that aren't as important, but which you would still like to spend time on, such as hobbies and interests, etc. When you have done this, you will have a clear list of your primary and secondary priorities that you can use to manage your time and your life more effectively.

Step 2: Schedule your time based on your priorities

Now take a further fifteen minutes and draw up a blank 'lifestyle grid' for your week which looks something like this:

	Mon	Tue	Wed	Thu	Fri	Sat	Sun
0700							
0800							
0900							
1000							
1100							
1200							
1300							
1400							
1500							
1600							
1700							
1800							
1900							
2000							
2100							
2200							

This lifestyle grid represents your entire week in one-hour slots, beginning at 7am and ending at 11pm each day. What you now need to do is allocate time for your personal necessities and primary priorities (which obviously includes time for your kids). Once you have done that, you can divide the time left over between your secondary priorities (hobbies and interests) and free time, which are basically blank segments that you can enjoy as you please. Including one free-time segment each day is a good idea as it will give your schedule some built-in flexibility that makes coping with emergencies and unexpected tasks a lot easier.

For example, let's say that you need to work from 8am to 4pm, Monday through to Friday, and that you also need to spend time with your children each day and with your partner to nurture and develop your relationship with her. Your secondary priorities are playing the banjo and maintaining your home on a DIY basis. With these priorities fresh in your mind, you might decide to schedule your time like this:

	Mon	Tue	Wed	Thu	Fri	Sat	Sun
0700							
0800	work	work	work	work	work	DIY	
0900	work	work	work	work	work	DIY	kids
1000	work	work	work	work	work	DIY	kids
1100	work	work	work	work	work	DIY	kids
1200	work	work	work	work	work	DIY	kids
1300	work	work	work	work	work	kids	
1400	work	work	work	work	work	kids	
1500	work	work	work	work	work	kids	
1600						kids	
1700	kids	kids	kids	kids	kids		
1800	kids	kids	kids	kids	kids		
1900	kids	kids	kids	kids	kids		
2000	banjo	banjo	banjo	banjo	banjo	partner	
2100	partner	partner	partner	partner	partner	partner	
2200							

You have now scheduled your time in such a way that you can spend three hours each day with your children, at least one hour alone each day with your partner and still have time to work and play your banjo. You've also ensured that you can take a half day on Saturday to spend on DIY and another half day with your kids. You can spend another half day with your kids on Sunday, and you have the rest of that day completely blank to use as you wish.

Of course, I realise that this particular pattern will not suit many people. Some of you will have to work longer hours, and maybe work six days a week instead of five. But this example isn't meant to be copied blindly. I provide it only so that you can see how scheduling your time using the lifestyle grid can help you organise your life more effectively based on your own personal list of priorities.

Having said this, I do believe that in most circumstances the great dad should try to adhere to a few basic minimums, and these are:

- Aim to spend at least one hour each day with your kids.

- Aim to spend at least one half-day block each week with your kids and partner.

- Aim to spend one whole weekend per month with your kids and partner.

- Aim to spend one whole week every three months with your kids and partner.

Why have I said 'and partner' in three of the above lines? Because children feel happiest when they are spending time with both of their parents together. If you can arrange this then your strength as a family unit will grow progressively stronger. Obviously, sometimes this just isn't possible. For example, many fathers don't actually live with their partner or their children. The good news is that this doesn't make it impossible to still be a great dad, and we will look at this particular topic in more detail in Chapter 19, Living Apart.

Step 3: Live by your schedule

At this stage you have consciously sorted out your priorities and scheduled your time accordingly using the lifestyle grid. The third step you need to take is to start living by your schedule, spending your time exactly as you have planned to spend it.

Now this is very simple in theory, but it can be difficult to achieve at first. Human beings are such habitual creatures that doing anything different initially feels awkward and artificial. The good news is that if you force yourself to adhere to your schedule for three consecutive weeks, you will find that a new habit has been established, and continuing to live this way will feel as natural as your current lifestyle does.

A very good by-product of living according to a lifestyle grid based on your personal priorities is that it will help you to achieve a healthier balance between your work and the rest of your life. Because you have scheduled time for your personal life, you will find that you are emotionally 'freed up' to perform better at work. And when you perform better at work, you will be more able to enjoy your personal life.

As you start living according to your lifestyle grid, be sure to focus only on the scheduled activity at hand. There's nothing worse than being at work and constantly thinking about all the stuff you have to do when you get home, only to get home and start thinking about everything you have to do when you get back to work. Aim to live as fully as possible in the present moment. When you're with your kids, enjoy being with your kids. When you're at work, enjoy being at work. Life is short, and spending much of it thinking about being somewhere else will only frustrate you. Being 'in the moment' and focusing on the experience at hand, by comparison, will enable you to squeeze a great deal of happiness out of each day – and provide a wealthy bank of memories which you can enjoy in your old age.

A word on quality time

So far, we have discussed how to give your child a quantity of time. But now we need to address the equally important topic of quality. Quality time is time that is scheduled for a specific purpose. It makes the time you spend with your kids more enjoyable because it is more productive than simply 'kicking back' and having fun.

Aim to make at least a quarter of the time you spend with your child each week quality time. Plan to do things together – to play a sport, go to the park, visit a museum, take a day trip, go to the cinema, and so on. When you share experiences like these with your child, it is easy for him or her to see that you really enjoy living in an involved way, rather than simply 'being there' as a detached spectator.

And if you can't think of anything particular to do? Ask your child. Children are infinitely creative and can generally come up with at least a dozen ideas before pausing for breath.

Teaching time management to your children

Your children will learn a lot about how to manage their own time by observing how you manage yours. If you manage your time consciously and deliberately, as we have just discussed, then these habits will go a long way to teaching your children to do the same.

In addition to this teaching by example, there are other ways of helping your children to learn to manage their own time more effectively that you might consider using:

Ages 0 to 5

Young children appreciate structure and repetition far more than most people realise. They like to know what to expect each day – not so that every day is exactly the same, but so that there are key elements that are fairly standard and predictable. Because of this, you should aim to establish some simple routines and patterns. Have set times for waking up, having meals, taking a bath and going to bed. This will provide your child with a sense of security and safety – and provide you as a parent with a sense of organisation.

Ages 6 to 10

As your children get older, help them to establish their own schedules for doing things such as cleaning their rooms, doing homework or watching TV. By giving them more control over the way they use their time, you can educate them about how time itself is limited and needs to be organised consciously if it is to be used effectively.

Ages 11 to 15

At this stage you can get your children to create a simple version of the lifestyle grid used earlier in this chapter. Get them to make a list of their own priorities (having fun, doing homework, playing with friends, going to school clubs, etc.) and create a complete lifestyle grid that will enable them to do all the things they want to do in any given week. If good time management is developed as a habit at this point in their lives, the chances are that they will continue to use it – or at least their own version of it – throughout the future.

Ages 16 to 20

By now, your children will probably know how to manage time effectively. What they may need more help with is in figuring out what is important and what isn't so important. We all want to do more things than we have time for, so your job here will be to help your children focus on priorities as they make some fairly major decisions concerning study, work and lifestyle.

When all is said and done, we have to remember that time can never be conquered, it can only be managed. You should therefore expect to review your priorities and schedule on a regular basis – at least once every three months – so that you can accommodate your changing needs rather than try to force them to fit into your existing schedule.

SUMMARY OF CHAPTER 6

- Spending time with your children is important, and you need to give them plenty of it. Aim to give them at least one hour each day, one half-day block each week, one whole weekend each month and one whole week every three months.
- Great dads don't *find* the time to spend with their kids – they *make* time.
  - Step 1: Consciously organise your priorities so that you know what is really important to you.
  - Step 2: Create a lifestyle grid and schedule your time so that your primary priorities take precedence.
  - Step 3: Live according to your schedule. This can be difficult at first, but if you stick with it for three weeks you will find that it becomes habitual.
- Make sure that at least one-quarter of the time you spend with your kids each week is quality time. This is time scheduled for a specific purpose.

CHAPTER 7

Physical Health

The health of your child is your number one priority, so in this chapter we will be looking at those aspects of life that have an impact on health, and how to manage them effectively. We will not be discussing the cure of specific illnesses – things like the flu or measles are of course a natural part of growing up, and in these circumstances being a great dad basically means ensuring that your child gets the appropriate love and medical attention – but rather, the various ways in which we can help our kids to establish lifestyle habits that support their health over the long term. The 'lifestyle habits' I refer to are fairly simple, and are familiar to most people:

- a healthy diet
- regular exercise
- a healthy sleeping routine.

The problem for most parents is that kids don't often like to do healthy things, especially if they have already established opposing habits. It should go without saying that we don't want to turn our kids into health freaks – and thereby risk pushing them towards an unhealthy obsession – but there are things that we can do to help them adopt healthier habits and make the whole process painless, if not downright enjoyable.

A healthy diet

We all know that a nutritious and well-balanced diet is a central key to good health. The human body – whether it is seven years old or seventy years old – is a finely tuned machine, and the food we put into the physical system is the fuel that provides the energy required for the machine to run properly. If we put poor fuel into this 'physical machine' then it won't work as efficiently as it is designed to. But if we put quality fuel into the same machine by adopting a healthy diet, it will run more smoothly, provide more energy and reduce the risk of it breaking down in the future.

The question, of course, is: What exactly is a healthy diet? Well, there are many dozens of books claiming to offer us an answer, but despite all of the 'fad' diets that are promoted, a healthy diet is quite simple to define:

A healthy diet is a common sense balance between proteins and good carbohydrates. It is rich in fruits, vegetables and fibre and low in salt, sugar, saturated fats and artificial additives.

Convenience foods – meaning those that are pre-packed or processed in some way – are very popular with children of all ages (and with adults too), but many of them are so loaded with salt, sugar, fats and additives that excessive consumption can actually cause physical illness – at least over the long term. Some additives can also have negative psychological effects. For example, it has been shown that the excessive consumption of foods and drinks containing artificial colourings can make a child hyperactive.

This doesn't mean that you shouldn't ever let your child eat foods or drinks that fit into this category, but as a great dad you should certainly make sure that they are consumed in moderation, and not to excess.

Getting a child to eat a healthy diet – one rich in fruits, vegetables, fibre, etc. – isn't always easy. But it's far from impossible. Here are some pointers to help you:

- Give your child a healthy breakfast each morning. Many kids enjoy cereals, and in this case choose a cereal which is low in sugar and salt and high in fibre. If your child prefers something sweeter, you can make the cereal more acceptable by adding sliced banana, a handful of raisins or some organic honey.

● Serve at least one portion of fresh vegetables with every main meal. Fresh vegetables contain many more vitamins and minerals than their tinned or frozen equivalents. If your child will eat only one or two 'favourite' vegetables, then serving these at every meal is far better than serving none at all.

● If you must use pre-packaged 'ready meals' from time to time (and they are useful on a particularly busy day) go for healthy options that are low in fat, sugar and salt.

● Get into the habit of reading the nutritional information labels on the food you buy. Try to avoid foods containing a lot of saturated fats, hydrogenated vegetable oils, sugar, salt and artificial additives (E-numbers).

● Limit the number of sweets and cakes your child consumes. Opt for healthier dessert options such as yoghurts or fruit salads instead of chocolate cake. When you do have chocolate cake or something similar, choose one from the 'healthy eating' range at your supermarket.

● Encourage your child to drink fresh fruit juices rather than sugar-loaded fizzy drinks. Water is the best option by far, but we have to be realistic – few children will enjoy drinking water all day.

Introduce the above ideas slowly if your child has already established unhealthy eating habits, otherwise start as you mean to continue. Children tend to eat what they see their parents enjoying, so if you start adhering to these healthy diet guidelines yourself, you will probably find that your child soon begins to follow your example automatically.

Remember, the aim here is not to make healthy eating a religion. You don't want to make your children so self-conscious about diet that they become obsessed by it. Be sensible and aim for moderation in all things.

Dealing with a picky eater

There is a common belief that some children are picky eaters (only agreeing to eat certain foods) whilst others eat anything put in front of them. The truth is that most young children go through short phases where they can be classed as 'picky eaters', so in most cases there is nothing to be overly concerned about – they will often get bored and move on to other foodstuffs quite naturally. If your child refuses to eat anything other than a very narrow range of foods for several weeks, or you are at all concerned that this pickiness could be due to some underlying medical condition, visit your GP for specific advice.

Regular exercise

We all know that exercise is good for us, at least in theory. It raises the metabolism, which helps us to burn fat faster. It floods our system with oxygen. It increases the production of natural feel-good chemicals, known as endorphins. It strengthens our immune system. And, as if all of that isn't enough, those who exercise on a regular basis enjoy higher levels of energy than those who don't.

Unfortunately, many adults associate the word exercise with pain, gruelling effort, exhaustion and boredom. Because of this, many children do the same. Encouraging a child to exercise on a regular basis is therefore a lot harder if you actually call it exercise. Play is another word entirely. Play means having fun, being energetic, being alive. Kids want to play all the time, and would happily do so all day long if they were able to.

The art of getting children to exercise is therefore to avoid the word exercise and to instead encourage them to play physical games. For example, there are many enjoyable sports they can take part in that will provide them with all the exercise they need if they are played on a regular basis. Consider the following ideas:

● Swimming. This provides great all-round cardiovascular exercise in a very gentle, low-impact way. Of course, being able to swim is also a potentially life-saving skill that all children should learn at some point.

- Running. The idea of jogging won't appeal to many kids, but you can turn this form of exercise into a game by inviting your child to race you three times a week around a local running track.

- Trampolining. Kids love trampolines, and although it just looks like a lot of fun, it's really a very good form of exercise.

- Cycling. Like swimming, cycling provides low-impact cardiovascular exercise and also gives your child a very useful skill that he or she can benefit from for decades to come.

- Tennis and badminton. These sports provide an element of competition that most kids enjoy. There's nothing a child likes more than being able to beat dad hands-down.

- Team sports. Things like five-a-side football, netball, basketball and volleyball give kids a purpose to keep moving for a definite amount of time. Kids often don't even think of these sports as exercise – especially young ones – they just focus on winning.

By encouraging your children to take part in these activities, you will automatically be encouraging them to exercise. But remember that going swimming once a month isn't enough. For exercise to be of maximum benefit, it needs to be done for at least twenty minutes, three times a week. Of course, you can vary things to keep your child's interest. Kicking a ball around in the garden on Monday, trampolining on Wednesday and going for a swim at the weekend will ensure that your child never gets bored, and provides all the exercise necessary to be strong and healthy.

A healthy sleeping routine

The third essential for physical health is sleep. Scientists have spent decades trying to discover exactly why the human machine needs sleep in order to function effectively. Although they have been unable to provide a simple answer, we do know that sleep is necessary in order for the body to repair itself and replenish its energy reserves. Dreams are also said to play an important role in keeping us psychologically healthy, as the brain processes information gathered during waking hours.

The amount of sleep we need varies according to age. As we have already seen, newborn babies often spend up to sixteen hours a day sleeping. Between ages one and five, a child may need up to twelve hours sleep a day. By the time a child reaches school age, the average requirement is around ten hours a day.

You should note that these are all averages. Every child is an individual, so don't worry if your toddler sleeps for ten hours rather than twelve. The important thing is health and well-being. If your toddler is perfectly healthy and happy sleeping ten hours a day, that's fine.

The problem for most parents is actually getting their children to sleep in the first place. Young kids have bags of energy and view each day as a unique adventure. Going to bed brings an end to that adventure, so they often resist if they possibly can.

There are three things that you can do to help your child establish a healthy sleeping routine. The first is to try to establish the routine as early as possible in the child's life. I mentioned this in a previous chapter, but it really is important for you and your partner to discuss the topic and agree on a specific bedtime for your child. By doing this, the child grows up with a fixed routine in place, and is far less likely to argue about going to bed than if you were to declare bedtime at a different time each day.

Second, make the bedroom itself as comfortable and enjoyable as possible. How you do this will obviously depend on the age of your child and his or her personal interests. If your child is at all scared of the dark, place a low-powered nightlight in the room so that he or she can feel comfortable and safe. Young girls (not babies, for safety reasons) will usually appreciate having a soft doll to sleep with. Young boys might prefer luminous stars decorating the bedroom ceiling. As long as they are safe and feel happy and comfortable in their bedrooms, you can be as creative as you like here.

The third thing you can do is make going to bed enjoyable. Create a ritual out of the process. For example, you could give your child a glass of milk and a piece of fruit or a plain biscuit.

Then, with teeth brushed and bathroom duties over, get your child tucked up in bed and spend ten or fifteen minutes reading a bedtime story, or talking about all the fun things they'll do the next day. This kind of enjoyable routine will be a lot more appealing to your child than making a sudden transition from fun to no-fun, and will therefore tend to produce fewer arguments when bedtime arrives.

Coping with illness

All children get ill at some point, and this applies no matter how healthy they are in general terms. Things like colds, the flu and measles are common, and if your child manages to avoid all of these things then you will be very lucky indeed.

Because we care about our kids, it's easy to panic or become overly anxious when a child is ill. The problem here is that children pick up on adult anxiety very quickly, and if they think that we are overly concerned, they often start to panic themselves.

For this reason, the first thing you need to do when your child is ill is keep calm. Comfort your child and give assurance that the illness is just temporary and that he or she will feel better soon. Then visit your GP for a diagnosis and to obtain a prescription for suitable medicine if necessary. When you get back home, help your child to focus on something other than the illness. Watching television, reading comics and playing computer games are all allowable here, as they all help to distract your child from distressing symptoms.

Try to be extra-patient throughout the illness. This can be difficult, because kids tend to get ill at the most inconvenient times possible – but they didn't choose to do so and therefore can't be blamed. Better roll with the punches or you'll be stressed as well as inconvenienced.

SUMMARY OF CHAPTER 7

- The health of your child is your number one priority. Sound physical health requires a healthy diet, regular exercise and a healthy sleeping routine.
- A healthy diet is a common sense balance between proteins and good carbohydrates – one that is rich in fruits, vegetables and fibre and low in salt, sugar, saturated fats and artificial additives.
- Encourage your child to exercise (avoiding the word) by playing physical games and sports. Try to get your child to exercise in this way three times a week.
- Adopt a healthy sleeping routine as early in your child's life as possible. Make the routine fun and make bedtime as enjoyable and comfortable as you can.
- If your child becomes ill, keep calm. Your child will pick up on any anxiety you show, so don't allow yourself to appear overly worried, even if that is how you really feel.

CHAPTER 8

Psychological Health

If the physical health of our children should be our number one priority, their psychological health obviously comes a very close second. This aspect of parenthood wasn't even considered by most people fifty years ago, but today it's absolutely vital. As great dads, it's our job to raise confident, responsible and self-assured children who have the best possible chance of making their lives a success in the increasingly competitive atmosphere of the modern world. It sounds like a daunting task, I know, but in reality we can go a long way to achieving this goal by adhering to some fairly simple rules.

Five simple rules

Rule 1: Make your child feel loved

When human beings feel that they are loved and valued, they tend to be far happier, far more confident and far more emotionally stable than those who feel unloved and unappreciated. This much is common sense, but what is not commonly understood is the fact that children aren't mind-readers. We cannot expect them to 'know' that they are loved and valued unless we tell them so – both verbally and through our daily actions.

There are many men who, for one reason or another, don't feel able to say 'I love you' out loud. It could be that their own fathers didn't use the phrase. It could be that they themselves were brought up to believe that such open expression was a sign of weakness – of being too soft or too emotional. A few men feel that expressing love openly to their children will make them appear less masculine than those who choose to keep their feelings to themselves.

The problem with this kind of attitude is that kids often interpret silence and aloofness in a father to mean that he doesn't care about them. This is rarely the case, but that doesn't matter. As far as the child is concerned, even a seed of doubt in this area can lead to a great deal of anguish and distress in later life.

A good habit for us to establish is to tell our kids every time we say goodbye or goodnight that we love them. I don't want to be morbid, but none of us is going to live forever, and our time might come tomorrow just as easily as it might come at the age of eighty. By making 'I love you' our parting words to our children on a routine basis, we can live our lives confident that, no matter when our time comes, we will have said the most important thing we can ever say to them.

All of the rules in this chapter are important, but if you only live by one of them, it should be this one. Tell your kids regularly that you love them, then back up that statement with the way you speak with them, the way you interact with them, and the way you live.

Rule 2: Express belief in your child

Self-confidence is extremely important, because it gives us the courage to try new things, expand our horizons and risk failing from time to time in order to achieve success. Many people think that confidence is something we are born with, but this really isn't the case. All self-confidence, at least initially, stems from the praise and encouragement we get in our formative years. Having someone who expresses a positive belief in us – be it a parent, teacher or other influential figure – makes us start believing and having confidence in ourselves. Whilst it is perfectly possible to develop self-confidence in later life even without such early praise and encouragement, we should do all we can to ensure that our children have the best possible head start.

Expressing belief in your children means encouraging them to reach their full potential, whatever that might be. We can catch them doing things well, and praise them for it. We can tell them that they have the courage, strength and potential to pursue their goals and make things happen. We can teach them that the only form of failure in life worth worrying about is the failure to try in the first place.

In this respect, being a great dad is a lot like being a sports coach. A good boxing coach doesn't tell his client that he'll never be able to beat his opponent. Instead, he tells his client that he has the potential to beat anyone he wants to. Rather than catching his client doing something wrong, as in 'Your uppercut stinks!', he will suggest an alternative approach in order to help the boxer improve.

As great dads, we need to do the same. Believe in the unlimited potential of your child, and express your belief as and when the opportunities to do so arise.

Rule 3: Don't preach a philosophy of perfection

Having just said how important it is for us to express belief in our kids, we now need to make sure that we don't go overboard and demand that they always live up to their potential. There is a fine line between encouraging our kids to aim high and expecting them to make the mark every time, and if we cross that line we risk them thinking that they need to be perfect in order to win our approval.

Perhaps the easiest way of avoiding a philosophy of perfection is to be honest about our own imperfections without getting hung up on them. Some dads like to let their kids believe that they are Superman and can do anything. But we're not and we can't. By setting an example of striving to reach our own potential and being honest and open about our 'failures', we automatically let them know that missing the mark is par for the course, and nothing to get too worked up about.

Rule 4: Teach the principle of gratitude

Severe stress and dissatisfaction are negative emotions that are most commonly experienced by people who don't fully appreciate what they already have. Those who are grateful for the good in their lives, by comparison, tend to be a lot happier and a lot more content.

We can teach the principle of gratitude most effectively by first practising it ourselves. Think about all that you have and all the people you value in your life. Pause daily to feel grateful for all of this. You don't have to make this a formal procedure, just feel gratitude in whatever way is appropriate for you.

Once you have established this habit yourself, you can begin pointing out to your children all the things that they too have to be grateful for. Don't say 'Be grateful', but instead comment more specifically on how fortunate they are to have this, or that, or to have good friends and so many other people who love them.

This approach will help your children to view their lives in a positive and contented way, and thereby avoid falling into the common trap of feeling discontented by focusing exclusively on what everyone else has.

Rule 5: Encourage an external focus

This rule doesn't mean that we should encourage our kids to compare themselves with others, but rather that they should understand from an early age that we are social beings and that we have to try to get along with others in order to have a peaceful and happy life.

Teaching this principle is simply a matter of occasionally asking your child to think from the perspective of others. For example, if you have a nine-year-old who is always leaving her room in a mess for her mother to take care of, ask her to think about the situation from her mother's point of view. Does she think that her actions make mum feel good or bad? Do they make her feel valued or taken for granted?

When kids are prompted in this way, they often experience a sudden realisation of how their actions affect other people, and immediately act to rectify the situation. But they do need to be prompted until having this kind of external focus becomes habitual.

Why good communication is essential

Good communication between your children and yourself is essential, and there are several very important reasons why this is so:

- Many of the 'rules' we have just looked at require the ability to communicate honestly with your child. If you can't communicate well then applying those rules to the way you interact with your child (and the way your child interacts with other people and the world in general) will be far more difficult than it needs to be.

- If you don't communicate well with your child on a day-to-day basis, there is no reason for the child to believe that you will be willing to do so when he or she has something really important to talk about. However, if you are in the habit of communicating openly and honestly with your kids, they will feel comfortable approaching you about almost anything they need to discuss, from the very trivial things to the very important things.

- Kids who enjoy open and honest communication with their parents tend to have a lot more self-esteem and confidence and are generally a lot less anxious than those children who don't feel that they can speak openly with their parents.

Seven general principles

So much for the benefits of good communication, but how can we as great dads learn to become great communicators? Once again, this isn't rocket science. In fact, if we adopt a few general principles and adhere to them, good communication will develop automatically.

Principle 1: Create opportunities for communication

If you are always dashing around in one direction and your kids are always dashing off in the opposite direction, the chances of you ever finding the opportunity to communicate properly are pretty slim. Merely hoping that opportunities will arise is not good enough. You need to deliberately create opportunities for communication.

The easiest way to do this is to have dinner together. In a perfect world, it would be ideal to be able to sit down to a family dinner every evening. If you can't do this (because of work commitments, for example) then make sure you adopt the habit at the weekends. Having meals together gives everyone in the family a chance to talk about anything that is on their mind without making things awkwardly formal.

Principle 2: Be interested

Don't just expect your child to come running to you to share information. Most kids need a bit of prompting, at least until they are in the habit of communicating openly. You can invite them to talk about their lives by being genuinely interested. Ask them how their day at school went, how they are getting on with their friends, what they would like to do at the weekend, and so on. Once you've expressed your interest, most kids will take things from there.

Principle 3: Think before you speak

Sometimes we all say things – especially at times of emotional stress – that we later regret. Unfortunately, kids tend to hang on to every word we say. Calling your child stupid in the heat of the moment may be something you forget about a couple of minutes later. Your child, on the other hand, may start mentally replaying that outburst over and over again. This can obviously lower his or her self-esteem considerably.

Kids also take general statements and make them personal. For example, if you comment that the 'damn kids next door are always making too much noise', then your own child may interpret this to mean that you want him to be quiet all the time. That wasn't your intention, of course, but it's a fairly logical conclusion for your child to make.

To guard against things like this, get into the habit of thinking before you speak. Put everything you say to your kids in a positive light if at all possible. If you need to criticise a behaviour, do so by first commenting on something good you have noticed about the child's behaviour in other areas. Then criticise the poor behaviour itself, and not your child. Finally, end on a positive note by suggesting ways in which he or she can learn from this criticism and derive something good from it.

Principle 4: Give your full attention

When you are speaking with your child, give your full attention. Look the child in the eye and smile. This makes your child feel connected to you, and makes communication more effective. If you cannot give your full attention – perhaps because you are in the middle of cooking dinner or fixing the car – pause for a moment, make eye contact and explain your predicament. Then ask if it would be okay to discuss the matter over dinner or when you have finished. The child may want to continue chatting immediately, but if so then at least he or she will understand why you are not giving your undivided attention.

Principle 5: Listen

Communication is a two-way process, and we need to listen as well as talk. Learn this lesson fast, and make sure that you always make time to listen to your child's point of view as well as share your own. This will make your child feel respected, and confident that their opinion, even if it disagrees with yours, is worth listening to. Establishing this habit of non-judgemental listening when your kids are young will make it more likely that they will trust in your ability to listen without judgement when they go through puberty and adolescence.

Principle 6: Talk, don't preach

When you talk with someone, you share your point of view and the reasoning behind it. When you preach at someone, you simply tell them what to do, often without explaining why. Kids generally don't mind you explaining things, but they hate being told something and being expected to take your word as gospel just because you've said it. For this reason, try to avoid preaching and opt for talking instead. It's simply a lot more effective.

Principle 7: Don't expect 100 per cent agreement

Children are individuals, and because of this basic fact of life we can't reasonably expect them to agree with everything that we say. Expecting kids to agree with us 100 per cent of the time will only turn our communication into a fight where one of us wins and one of us loses.

It therefore makes sense to accept that disagreements are normal. Having your children disagree with you is a good sign that they are beginning to think independently and forming their own opinions, so don't get upset when it happens. Rather, feel proud of their willingness to go their own way and not blindly follow yours.

Adapting your communication skills

Having presented the seven principles of good communication, let's end this chapter by taking a brief look at how we should adapt our communication skills to meet the differing needs of our children during the four main stages of development.

Ages 0 to 5

At this age, kids relate more to our tone of voice and our gestures than they do to our words. We can therefore communicate more effectively if we exaggerate both of these things. For example, instead of saying 'You painted a really great picture there, Jimmy', with a straight face and a casual voice, try to express the idea in gestures and words at the same time. Smile wide, and talk as if he's just finished running a marathon. He'll respond far better to this kind of approach.

Ages 6 to 10

Kids begin to ask all sorts of questions during this stage, so make sure you take time to answer them as fully as you can, whenever this is appropriate. The common response of dismissing questions and asking kids to simply 'do as they are told' gives the impression that their (often perfectly reasonable) questions aren't important. Taking a few moments to answer them, on the other hand, indicates to the child that all questions are worthy of our time, and his or her self-esteem is boosted as a result.

Ages 11 to 15

You can expect communication to be more difficult during puberty and adolescence than at other times, but this doesn't mean it becomes impossible. At this stage, children are discovering what it means to be more and more independent, so they will start demanding more privacy, more space for themselves and more freedom to form their own opinions. As long as you are mindful of all this, allow your children to keep certain things to themselves and continue adhering to the seven principles outlined earlier, communication with your growing child shouldn't pose too many problems.

Ages 16 to 20

You're speaking with a young adult now and not a child, so don't expect the reactions typical of a child. It's often a good idea to think of how you might discuss a topic with a young man or woman of the same age who has just joined your company at work. Be as respectful, polite and amiable with your adult kids as you would be to a colleague of the same age.

SUMMARY OF CHAPTER 8

As great dads, it's our job to raise confident, responsible and self-assured children.

- There are five rules we can adhere to in order to achieve this:
  - Rule 1: Make your child feel loved.
  - Rule 2: Express belief in your child.
  - Rule 3: Don't preach a philosophy of perfection.
  - Rule 4: Teach the principle of gratitude.
  - Rule 5: Encourage an external focus.
- Good communication is also essential, and we can follow seven principles to help us become more effective in this area:
  - Principle 1: Create opportunities for communication.
  - Principle 2: Be interested.
  - Principle 3: Think before you speak.
  - Principle 4: Give your full attention.
  - Principle 5: Listen.
  - Principle 6: Talk, don't preach.
  - Principle 7: Don't expect 100 per cent agreement.

CHAPTER 9

Education

When all is said and done, the overall responsibility of a great dad is to educate his children. He must educate them about how to eat healthily, how to take care of their bodies through exercise, how to feel confident, how to get along with others, and so on. But children need much more education than we as parents can provide ourselves, especially if they are to succeed as adults in the competitive world of industry and commerce. That's why formal education – which primarily teaches intellectual knowledge rather than life skills – is so essential to their development.

Formal education

At one time, children didn't join the school system until they really had to by law. Today, education is recognised as being so fundamentally important that sending kids to nurseries and pre-schools is very common. The advantage of sending your child to a good nursery or pre-school is that it establishes a pattern of being away from Mum and Dad and helps to develop some basic social skills – such as playing with a variety of other kids from a wide range of backgrounds – at an early age.

Formal education usually begins at the age of five in most parts of the UK, with many primary schools (particularly in Wales) inviting children of a younger age to join preparatory reception classes. If your child has attended nursery or pre-school then the transition to primary should be fairly smooth, but don't expect it to be totally comfortable. Some kids are so attached to their parents that they will literally kick and scream in protest for the first few days. This is obviously upsetting when it happens, but attending primary for the first time is a rite of passage that all children have to go through, so if your child reacts in this way, take comfort from the fact that the tears and tantrums do go away once the habit of attendance has been established.

At primary school your child will learn the fundamentals – reading, writing and arithmetic – as well as basic science, history, geography, etc. Your child will be introduced to the concept of homework and to the idea of being responsible for his or her own learning. There may also be the opportunity to take part in some extra-curricula activities, such as playing as part of a football or netball team.

Your child will attend primary school up to the age of eleven before moving on to a secondary school. This builds on primary school education and goes much further. Your child will now study mathematics, computer science, chemistry, physics, art, drama, English literature, and so on. As your child progresses through the secondary system, there will be the opportunity to choose between certain subjects according to personal preferences. For example, a child may choose between studying art or learning a second language, such as French or German. Whilst you can obviously help and support your child in making these decisions, you need to remember that the decisions themselves are his or hers to make.

Secondary school education ends at the age of sixteen, and culminates with examinations in the subjects studied. The better the exam results gained here, the more choice your child will have when it comes to deciding on what to do next, so do make sure that you treat this stage of education with the respect it deserves.

Once a child reaches the age of sixteen there is no obligation to continue with formal education if this isn't desired. However, continuing education after secondary school is a good idea for many kids, so raising your child with an expectation of going on to study for A-levels at college and then for a degree at university is not a bad approach to take. After all, your child can always choose not to do this when getting to that stage, so assuming further education from the outset isn't harmful in the least – as long as you do ultimately allow your son or daughter to make the decision on this matter when the time comes.

Helping your child to thrive

Although children up to the age of sixteen receive most of their formal education from primary and secondary schools, this doesn't mean that we as great dads can sit back and forget about it. On the contrary, we need to do whatever we can to support the formal education system and thereby help our kids to thrive rather than simply get by. Here's how.

Principle 1: Encourage positive homework habits

Your child will begin to be set homework during their time at primary school. The work itself will obviously be quite easy at this stage, and will usually take no more than an hour each week to complete. But it is important that we use it to help our kids establish positive habits that will serve them well in later years.

First, try to provide a place where your child can do homework without interruption. It could be at a small desk in his or her own bedroom or, if this isn't possible, at the dining room table. Just make sure that you don't allow the television or CD player droning away in the background, because unnecessary external stimuli will obviously reduce the child's ability to concentrate.

Next, help your child to establish a regular homework routine so that it is attended to at the same time each week. If you leave it to your child to get organised, the homework could well end up being done at the last minute or not at all. Teaching the value of setting aside a specific time for a specific task on a regular basis (as we saw with your time management) will not only help the child as far as homework is concerned, but in many other areas of life as well.

Be supportive and helpful when your child comes to you for assistance, but don't do the homework yourself. It is often very tempting to simply answer a question because it only takes a moment, but in the longer term it's far more beneficial to spend a little more time helping a child to think things through. For example, if your child asks you 'What is 12 times 8?' you shouldn't immediately come back with the answer of 96. Instead, encourage him or her to break the problem down into stages. Ask 'What is 10 times 8?' and wait for an answer. Then ask 'So if 10 times 8 equals 80, what do you think 12 times 8 is?' You might spend several minutes working towards the right answer – but by taking this more time-consuming approach your child will learn to arrive there fairly independently.

In the early years of primary school, when your children are only just learning to read properly, it makes sense that they should come to you for help and support with their homework. However, as soon as they are proficient at reading, you should start encouraging your children to turn to reference books for answers to difficult questions. For example, if your child wants to spell the word 'significant', invest some time in teaching how to use a dictionary. There are many excellent dictionaries and reference books available for children of all ages, so teaching your children to refer to these as a first port of call will help to establish a habit that should serve them well for a lifetime.

As your child enters and progresses through secondary school, homework will be more frequent, more substantial and more challenging. Secondary schools assume that, by now, the habit of doing homework effectively has been established, so from the beginning your child will be expected to do a fair amount of it. It's a good idea to help kids re-organise their schedules to accommodate this additional workload, and to encourage them to spend a specific amount of time each day on homework rather than building up a daunting backlog for the weekend.

Principle 2: Encourage learning for fun

Many kids grow up thinking that learning is boring – especially if they only associate learning with dry textbooks and school lessons. It's your job to teach them that this is only one form of learning, and that there are many other ways to learn things – ways that can be enjoyable, fun and entertaining. How do you do this? You have a number of options available to you:

- Take your child to a museum, art gallery or exhibit which matches his or her personal interests. Many museums and galleries organise days that are specifically designed to attract and entertain children, so keep up to date with what's available and then take your child along as a special treat. (Note that calling it a special treat will go down a lot better than calling it an additional day of education.)

- When buying gifts for your child, say for birthdays and Christmas, try to include at least one that has some definite educational value. Telescopes, chemistry sets, interactive computer programs and so on are all popular with children. Just make sure that you buy a gift that is suitable in terms of age and ability. If it's too basic the child will get bored, and if it's too advanced he or she will get frustrated.

- Don't assume that *all* television is chewing gum for the brain. There are many TV programmes with enormous educational value. Take the CBBC programme Newsround, for example, or virtually any of the content on the Discovery Kids satellite channel. Introducing kids to this kind of programming isn't very difficult, and as long as you don't force the issue (always remember, kids need encouragement, not commands) they can learn a lot even when they are watching TV.

- Encourage your child to read for pleasure. Books are the greatest source of knowledge that we have (the Internet included), but unless children have first established the habit of reading for pleasure they are unlikely to read much non-fiction. The best way I have found to create an interest in books in my own children is to start with titles that tie-in with their favourite television or computer games characters. Kids are generally keen to read magazines, comics and books featuring familiar characters and situations, so using these as a springboard into a wider range of fiction, then non-fiction, puts this natural enthusiasm to good use.

Principle 3: Teach your child to think independently

There are many people who believe that children should just accept what they are taught as it is given, and never question the opinion of those in authority. Unfortunately, those who go along with this philosophy tend to raise kids who are often capable but seldom original.

Teaching your child to think independently is, in my opinion, a much better way forward. By encouraging kids to ask difficult questions and find the accompanying answers, they not only become more interested in various subjects, but they also tend to learn much faster and to a much greater depth because of that increased interest. For example, a secondary school student who questions why democracy is a good thing (as opposed to communism, let's say) will gain a much better understanding of the subject than a student who simply agrees with the teacher as a matter of course and without doing any independent thinking.

You can teach your child to think independently by encouraging the asking of questions on a regular basis, and by also encouraging the finding of answers with the help of reference books and by asking school teachers for more information. Both approaches, taken simultaneously, will help your child to take more responsibility for his or her own education and, in all probability, to take more responsibility in life as a whole.

Helping a child to cope with peer pressure

Human beings are social beings, so it should come as no surprise that children – like the rest of us – feel a basic, instinctive need to be accepted and approved of by a larger group. In order to meet this need, individuals tend to do whatever they can to 'fit in' with everyone else. They listen to the same kinds of music, adopt the same kinds of phrases when speaking, adopt the same kind of hobbies and enjoy wearing the same kind of clothes. This, in a nutshell, is what peer pressure is all about – the invisible pressure to fit in with peers.

Peer pressure gets a lot of bad press, but the fact is that a lot of peer pressure is relatively harmless. It doesn't really matter if a girl or boy listens to Gareth Gates or Will Young, or supports Manchester United or Chelsea. What matters is when peer pressure encourages young children to lie, cheat or steal, or older ones to smoke, drink, have underage sex and experiment with drugs. At this stage, unless we have taught our kids otherwise, they will often feel compelled to do whatever it takes to continue 'fitting in' with the larger group.

The key to helping a child to cope with peer pressure is therefore very simple: discuss the subject before it becomes a problem. By providing your child with an objective understanding of what peer pressure is all about, you effectively help him or her to see the wood for the trees, and to recognise what is happening as it happens.

Another good way of teaching kids about peer pressure is to tell stories about your own childhood when you did something stupid to try to fit in with your own school friends. Make yourself look really dumb in these stories, and appear embarrassed even as you tell them. If you do this, your child will quickly associate giving in to unreasonable peer pressure with the emotions of stupidity and embarrassment. This sounds rather harsh, but because you are talking about yourself, it won't come across as if you're preaching in any way, shape or form. On the contrary, most kids will choose to avoid giving in to unreasonable peer pressure if only to avoid being as dumb as dad was. Yes, you will feel like a jerk doing this, but great dads are willing to feel like jerks if the long-term payoff is a better future for their kids.

Studies have shown that peer pressure is normally worse for those kids who have low self-esteem and low self-confidence, and this is not surprising. The less self-esteem a child has, the more he or she will feel the need to be accepted by peers. If you apply the principles you learned in the previous chapter then this shouldn't be a problem.

Helping a child to cope with bullying

We should address the topic of bullying here because many experts believe it is closely related to peer pressure. It occurs when one or two individuals choose to intimidate – either verbally or physically – a specific student in order to impress their particular peer group. Bullying at any age should never be ignored. Nor should a child be told simply to stand up for himself or herself.

Instead, the following advice, published by the British government, should be followed as closely as possible as soon as you discover that your child is being bullied. The following information is © Crown copyright:

- *Calmly talk with your child about his or her experience.*

- *Make a note of what your child says, particularly who was said to be involved; how often the bullying has occurred; where it happened and what has happened.*

- *Reassure your child that he/she has done the right thing to tell you about the bullying. Explain to your child that should any further incidents occur he/she should report them to a teacher immediately.*

- *Make an appointment to see your child's class teacher or form tutor and explain to the teacher the problems your child is experiencing. When talking with teachers about bullying, try to stay calm. Bear in mind that the teacher may have no idea that your child is being bullied or may have heard conflicting accounts of an incident. Be as specific as possible about what your child says has happened, give dates, places and names of other children involved.*

- *Make a note of what action the school intends to take. Ask if there is anything you can do to help your child or the school. Stay in touch with the school; let them know if things improve as well as if problems continue.*

Of course, all of this assumes that your child is the one being bullied. But what if you find out that it's your child doing the bullying? In this case the following guidelines are issued:

- *Talk with your child. Explain that what he or she is doing is unacceptable and makes other children unhappy.*

- *Discourage other members of your family from bullying behaviour or from using aggression or force to get what they want.*

- *Show your child how he/she can join in with other children without bullying.*

- *Make an appointment to see your child's class teacher or form tutor and explain the problems your child is experiencing. Discuss with the teacher how you and the school can stop him or her bullying others.*

- *Regularly check with your child how things are going at school.*

- *Give your child lots of praise and encouragement when he or she is co-operative or kind to other people.*

SUMMARY OF CHAPTER 9

- The overall responsibility of a great dad is to educate his children. We need to do whatever we can to support the formal education system and thereby help our kids to thrive rather than simply get by. We can do this in three main ways:
  - Principle 1: Encourage positive homework habits.
  - Principle 2: Encourage learning for fun.
  - Principle 3: Teach your child to think independently.
- A certain amount of peer pressure is normal and relatively harmless. However, it can become unreasonable. You should discuss the subject with your child before it becomes a problem so that he or she is able to recognise and deal with such unreasonable pressure.
- Bullying should never be ignored or dismissed as being unimportant. Instead, follow the guidelines issued by the British government, as described in this chapter.

CHAPTER 10

Recreation

Many parents think that recreation – playing with toys, having hobbies and interests, playing games, and so on – is just a fun way for kids to pass the time. However, the truth is that recreation also plays a very important role in child development, with different forms of recreation each offering specific benefits. For example:

- Playing games teaches kids about rules and provides an opportunity for them to experience both winning and losing. Team games, such as football, also help a child to develop social skills and learn the importance of working as part of a larger group.

- Artistic play, such as drawing and painting, helps children to develop their creativity. It also helps them to develop their sense of colour and perspective as well as improve hand-to-eye coordination.

- Constructive play, which includes building blocks, using Lego and making models, helps kids improve hand-to-eye coordination and develops their ability to think more logically.

- Pretend play, both with props (such as playing with a doll or toy car) and without props (such as playing a Harry Potter inspired game of 'Wizards and Witches' in the playground) helps children to develop their imaginative skills, as well as make greater distinctions between fantasy and reality.

- Puzzle play, such as jigsaws, word games and number games, helps kids to develop their cognitive skills and their ability to think more logically.

This list is by no means exhaustive. Recreation also helps children to improve their levels of literacy, numeracy and communication skills, and in some cases even their physical health and fitness. It's therefore clear that, far from simply being a fun way to pass the time, recreation is essential to the healthy overall development of our kids.

As great dads, it's our job to encourage our kids to explore all possible forms of recreation as they grow. They won't take to all of them with equal enthusiasm, and that's to be expected because we all have our personal likes and dislikes. However, by providing them with plenty of recreational options, they are certain to find something they enjoy, and the likelihood of them complaining of boredom is much reduced.

What's appropriate?

The key to helping children get the most out of recreation is to offer options that are relevant to their age and level of ability. If we don't do this then kids will either get bored (as would be the case if we gave a rattle to a twelve-year-old) or frustrated (as would happen if we gave a chess set to a two-year-old.) To help guide you in the selection of suitable and relevant options, here are some suggestions based on the four age ranges used throughout this book.

Note that you should always check to make sure that any toy/activity offered to your child is safe for his or her age. All toys legally sold in the UK have a recommended age, such as 3 + or 0–6 months. Adhering to these guidelines is the best way to ensure your child's safety.

Ages 0 to 5

The recreation options for a young baby are obviously very limited. Choose mobiles that have been safety approved for the age of your child and which provide visual and possibly also auditory stimulation. Apart from this, you can entertain your child by doing what parents have done for centuries – by pulling funny faces and making funny noises. Once your child can grip things, you can also introduce simple toys such as rattles.

Toddlers and pre-schoolers are increasingly well catered for in the toy department. Manufacturers now recognise the huge educational role that toys can play in the life of a child, so there are a wide variety of options available for children aged 6 months to 3 years. A special word of recommendation should go towards toys that provide some kind of feedback, such as those that play a tune or light up when a button is pushed. These will teach your child the basics of cause and effect. Giving your child push-button and 'toddler-friendly' books is a good way of introducing the concept of reading even before the child is actually ready to do so. Rudimentary games, such as rolling a ball or playing catch, can also be introduced in due course.

As your child gets older, the complexity of toys will need to gradually increase in order to maintain both their appeal and their educational value. Games that bring the imagination into play, such as tea-sets, dolls, dressing-up outfits, and so on, will be popular at this stage. Simple jigsaws will help your child to improve hand-to-eye coordination and logical thinking processes. Any opportunity you can provide for children to play together, such as at a nursery or reception class, will also be very beneficial.

Ages 6 to 10

Between the ages of 6 and 10, children progress rapidly as far as recreation is concerned. They will be able to handle increasingly complex puzzles and games of all kinds, such as card games, board games and memory games. They will probably enjoy watching television, going to the cinema and playing computer or video console games. Whilst these are all perfectly valid forms of entertainment when allowed in moderation, you will have to guard against permitting your child to become a couch potato.

At the beginning of this stage, your child can be introduced to overtly social forms of recreation by joining popular organisations such as the Brownies or Cub Scouts. These are excellent for encouraging a child's social development, and they also tend to have a high degree of educational content, so do give this option serious consideration.

This is also a good time to get your child enthusiastic about the kinds of recreation which promote good health, as discussed in Chapter 7.

Ages 11 to 15

As your child goes through puberty and adolescence, their social lives will probably play a big role in the types of recreation they enjoy. He or she will want to visit friends, go to parties and participate in sports with peers. All of this is important, as it helps your son or daughter to develop social skills even further – but your job as a great dad is still not over in this area. Aim to help your child enjoy a balance of recreational options, some involving peers, some with the family, and some that can be enjoyed alone.

Children in this age bracket are often tempted to drink, smoke, experiment with drugs and have underage sex because they think that these activities will make them feel more grown-up. A good way to reduce the power of such temptations is to introduce your child to a variety of positive and healthy 'adult' recreational options such as dining out with the family, going ten-pin bowling or ice-skating, and visiting the cinema. Then, when your child feels the urge to be 'grown-up', he or she is just as likely to go bowling or watch a movie as to light up a Marlboro or sneak into the local pub. Of course, this doesn't mean that the unhealthy options will never be experimented with – it would be unrealistic to think that we can ever totally protect our children from their own curiosity. But it does mean that your kids won't experiment for lack of alternative choices.

Music tends to play an increasingly important part of life for children at this stage of their lives, because their choice of band, artist or performer can help them to strengthen their own identity. Even if you don't have the same taste in music as your child does, recognise that it's a fairly innocuous form of recreation and therefore not something that normally needs to be discouraged unless the lyrical content itself is inappropriate. For example, letting an eleven-year-old listen freely to the latest

Girls Aloud CD is fine, but allowing the same level of freedom with the latest Eminem album is probably unwise because of the very explicit lyrical content. Apply common sense to this matter – listen to an album yourself to help you make an informed decision if necessary – and don't simply forbid music on the basis of (your) taste.

Ages 16 to 20

By now your child will be making most decisions about recreation, so your role will primarily be support and encouragement. Having said this, you should still try to have fun with your kids on a fairly regular basis if they are still living at home. It could be a game of tennis or squash every week, or a meal at a restaurant once a month. Just don't expect to feature in their recreational activities as a matter of course. Your kids now have friends of their own and are making the legal transition from childhood to adulthood – so be prepared to take much more of a back seat if that's what your kids want you to do.

Whilst I have gone to some lengths to suggest various ways in which you can encourage your child to make the most of recreational options, you should not come away from this chapter with the idea that you have to organise everything. Your child also needs space to grow, so you must provide a certain amount of freedom that will naturally increase as he or she gets older. Allowing some freedom gives your child the opportunity to find unique ways of having fun, and to have fun spontaneously as well as in a more structured way – as happens when you arrange a weekly swim session, for example.

Holidays

Children love holidays, and if you've been paying attention to previous chapters you'll have a good idea why. Holidays take you away from your work responsibilities and give you plenty of free time – time to spend generously with your kids.

As far as kids are concerned – younger ones especially – the holiday destination itself is secondary to the benefit of them being able to spend a lot more time with you. Many families are therefore able to enjoy very good holidays without the hassle and expense of a long-haul flight, and quite a few don't even bother going abroad.

What you need to remember is that a family holiday should do three things:

- It should give you plenty of time to enjoy with your kids.

- It should give you plenty of opportunities to do new things in a new environment.

- It should be fun for the whole family.

Note that constant sunshine, exotic locations, first-class accommodation and 24-hour room service are all optional extras, not necessities. If you can find a resort in the UK that will give you a week or two with the kids, offers plenty of things to do and which the whole family will enjoy, go for it. By the same token, if taking a long-haul flight to an exotic location will instantly wipe out two days of your holiday, put you under a great deal of stress (either mental or financial) and leave you all with nothing to do except swim and sunbathe once you get there, think again. A good holiday is one that is genuinely enjoyed, not one that simply costs the most and boasts the best temperature.

With that important distinction made, here are some suggestions on how to get the most out of your family holidays for each of the four age ranges.

Ages 0 to 5

First, choose a destination that is convenient for both you and your partner. Up to the age of five, your child probably won't be able to tell the difference between Disneyland Paris and Disneyworld in Orlando, Florida, so go for an option that is easiest for you. Take plenty of supplies (nappies, favourite foods, etc.) if you are at all doubtful about their availability at the destination. If sunscreen is going to be at all necessary, use one manufactured for babies and toddlers, because adult sunscreen just won't give a child's sensitive skin enough protection from harmful UV rays.

Perhaps the most stressful aspect of a holiday with a child in this age bracket is the travelling. Kids get bored very easily when travelling for more than half an hour, so take a few small toys to keep them occupied for the duration of the journey. Also make sure that you plan for regular rest breaks so that they can go to the toilet and stretch their legs.

Ages 6 to 10

As well as wanting to be with you, kids of this age will be interested in what they will be able to do at the chosen destination. This doesn't automatically mean that you need to spend more on your holiday, but that you need to choose a location that will entertain and occupy your children as well as yourself. For example, if swimming is popular with your kids, it makes sense to look for a place with a pool. The advice given a moment ago about sunscreen and keeping the kids occupied on the journey also applies here.

Many family holiday destinations, both in the UK and abroad, have clubs for children which are specifically designed to entertain them as well as giving them the opportunity to make new friends. These clubs tend to be very popular with kids and can give their leisure time a bit of structure, so do look into any that are offered at your location.

Ages 11 to 15

Kids will begin wanting to do their own thing as they progress through this age bracket, so before booking your holiday try to ensure that they will be able to do so safely. Choosing holiday destinations with on-site sporting and recreational facilities is usually a good idea.

Because they are older, kids are now generally prepared to travel for longer if the payoff is going to be worth it. If you've always wanted to fly long-haul as a family and explore more distant locations, this is probably the time to do so. However, the boredom of travelling won't have disappeared altogether, so make sure they have at least one good book and a personal stereo to keep them busy when the in-flight entertainment proves lacking.

Ages 16 to 20

Now you may find that your kids aren't very interested in family holidays. Instead they may be talking about going away with friends, or staying behind at home while you go away with your partner. Because kids are at different levels of maturity at (for example) age sixteen, you should exercise common sense in this matter. Don't insist that they come with you; but at the same time don't give them free reign to travel the globe with their friends. Always remember that, until they reach the age of eighteen, your kids are not legally adults, so you are still very much responsible for them.

If your kids are still interested in taking a family holiday with you, it's often a good idea to get their input when choosing a destination. Discuss the budget available, then allow them to make suggestions. You never know, maybe your kids will try to broaden your horizons.

SUMMARY OF CHAPTER 10

- Recreation plays a very important role in child development, with different forms of recreation each offering specific benefits.
- As great dads, it's our job to encourage our kids to explore all possible forms of recreation as they grow.
- The key to helping a child get the most out of recreation is to offer options that are relevant to his or her age and level of ability.
- As well as needing some elements of organised recreation, your child also needs space to grow, so you must provide a certain amount of freedom that will naturally increase with time.
- Family holidays provide a great opportunity to experience extended times of recreation. The important point to remember is that a family holiday should do three things:
  - It should give you plenty of time to enjoy with your kids.
  - It should give you plenty of opportunities to do new things in a new environment.
  - It should be fun for the whole family.

CHAPTER 11

Discipline

The subject of disciplining children is an emotive one. Hardly a month goes by without some discussion of it appearing in the newspapers or in the schedules of radio and television news programmes, and almost every parent has a view as to what makes some forms of discipline right and what makes some forms of discipline wrong.

Fifty years ago it was common for a parent to physically smack a child and for school teachers to cane or slipper unruly pupils as a way of punishing poor behaviour. Whether this was ever effective or not is still being disputed – it is my opinion that any short-term benefit that might have been observed was greatly outweighed by long-term consequences. In the modern world it's a moot point. Schools are no longer allowed to use corporal punishment and, according to recently introduced laws in the UK, parents are no longer allowed to smack a child with such force that a mark is left on the skin. This is, in many ways, a rather vague law, and it would not be surprising to see it revised in the future – perhaps making any physical punishment of children illegal.

As great dads, I believe we shouldn't feel the need to wait for a law to change before adopting a general 'no smack' policy. Imagine being pulled over by a traffic cop and punched in the face because you exceeded the limit and you'll understand just how crazy it is to try to teach a kid to learn right from wrong by causing physical pain.

Some parents think that smacking is an appropriate form of punishment. I don't agree. I think this belief is held only by those who have a mistaken understanding of what discipline is all about. Discipline is not something that we dish out in order to punish bad behaviour. It is a tool we need to use carefully and compassionately in order to teach our kids that their actions have consequences.

Five principles of discipline

Children are fairly easy to discipline as long as certain sensible principles are adhered to. Let's now look at those principles so that you can begin to apply them in your own life.

Principle 1: Discipline from a place of love, not anger

Although poor behaviour in our kids can often make us feel angry, it is generally not a good idea to discipline a child unless we feel fairly objective. The aim should not be to scare the hell out of our kids by throwing a tantrum of our own, but to discipline them in a calm and fair way so that they benefit from the experience. If you can't proceed in this way – and sometimes our emotions take a while to fade – then tell your child that he or she will be disciplined for bad behaviour but should go to the bedroom until you have had a chance to calm down. And how do you calm down in such a short space of time? Try these ideas:

● Take twenty slow, deep breaths, or close your eyes and meditate for five minutes.

● Think about the big picture. Will this particular incident be fairly insignificant one year, five years or ten years from now? Will you eventually laugh about it? If the answer to these questions is yes, why not choose to feel calmer about it now?

● Imagine that you and your child have swapped places. As the child, what are you thinking? What are you concerned about? How would you like your father to address the situation in a way that still makes you feel loved and cared for?

● Pick up this book and read this chapter again.

These are all simple ideas, but they can be very effective in helping you to let go of the emotion of anger and leave you in a much calmer state of mind so that you can discipline your child from a place of love.

Principle 2: Verbally identify what your child did wrong

We have considered the importance of communication a number of times, but in the area of disciplining our children it is absolutely essential, because unless we communicate exactly what it is that our children have done wrong they will never be able to learn from their mistakes and behave more properly in the future. Without proper communication, we'd end up with something like this:

PARENT: Alright, that's it! Go to your room and don't come down until I say so!

CHILD: Why? What have I done?

PARENT: You know damn well what you've done, so you can just go to your room and think about why it's important that you don't do it again!

Confused, the kid goes up to his room. Twenty minutes later, he calls downstairs ...

CHILD: Is it all right if I come back down now?

PARENT: Have you learned your lesson?

CHILD: Uhm... yeah... I think so...

Now you might think that this is a little far-fetched, but this kind of thing happens all the time across the nation. Kids are being punished without any explicit communication of the behaviour that has merited the punishment. In some cases, of course, the child is well aware of what he or she did to deserve the punishment, but in many other cases children are confused. And if they're confused about what it is that they did wrong, the chances of them correcting their behaviour in the future are slim.

The second principle of good discipline is therefore fairly simple: before disciplining your child always ensure that he or she understands exactly what it is that they did wrong. And remember, you should focus on criticising the poor behaviour more than the child.

Principle 3: Explain the consequences of the poor behaviour

As we have already said, discipline is meant to teach children that their actions have consequences. Having explained exactly what it is that the child did wrong, you should now explain the consequences of the poor behaviour. For example:

PARENT: Okay, so why am I angry?

CHILD: Because I called Auntie Ethel an old fart during dinner?

PARENT: That's right. And do you know why that's not a good thing to do?

CHILD: Because it's wrong to call people old?

PARENT: Because calling someone an old fart hurts their feelings. You wouldn't want people to call you names, would you?

CHILD: No.

A good way to convey the inevitable consequences of poor behaviour is to encourage the child to use his or her own reasoning. Ask directly what the consequences are of touching a hot stove, throwing stones at the neighbour's window or writing 'Clean Me' in the dirt on your employer's Mercedes. By giving your children the opportunity to identify the consequences for themselves – and elaborating as necessary – the logic of why certain behaviours are not acceptable will be remembered for much longer than if you simply preached for five minutes.

Principle 4: Decide on the appropriate form of discipline

If the government were to suddenly announce that all crimes – no matter how large or small – would attract the same sentence of life imprisonment, society would be outraged. There's something within us all that instinctively knows that any form of punishment needs to be appropriate to the crime committed in order for it to be genuinely fair.

The same principle applies to disciplining children. In order for us to discipline them fairly, we need to make sure that the type of discipline used is determined only by the severity of the misbehaviour, and not by the fact that we ourselves are in a particularly bad mood.

This approach is a lot easier to adhere to if we have consciously decided on various 'levels' of disciplining that we will use in certain circumstances. To give you some idea of what I mean, consider these five levels of discipline which I use with my own children:

- *Level One – the verbal warning.* In my opinion, everyone deserves a second chance, especially for a first offence. That's why my Level One form of discipline is to give my kids a verbal warning. I don't simply give them an ear-bashing, but try to explain why a certain type of behaviour is wrong or inappropriate. I help my kids to identify the consequences of their actions and to tell me whether or not I'm being fair in drawing attention to the poor behaviour. Then I will ask them to refrain from repeating the same poor behaviour in the future. In many cases, that's as far as discipline needs to go.

- *Level Two – restitution.* This is where I discipline my kids by making them 'pay off' any debt caused by their bad behaviour. If they make a mess, they clear it up. If they upset someone, they take steps to make them feel better. This approach teaches kids that undoing the consequences brought on by misbehaviour is often a lot more hassle than simply avoiding the misbehaviour in the first place.

- *Level Three – time out.* Sometimes all it takes for a child to learn that misbehaviour has negative consequences is for us to demand that they take time out. I've sent my kids to their rooms for periods of ten minutes, twenty minutes and – at its most extreme – an hour. This gives them time to think about their behaviour and to calm down when they're feeling particularly angry or upset.

- *Level Four – the ban.* If a previous 'misdemeanour' is repeated consistently and deliberately (and not just because my kids, like all others, can be absent-minded at times) I take my discipline to Level Four. This involves a ban of some sort, but the nature and length of the ban are determined by the type and severity of the misdemeanour. Sometimes I'll ban my kids from watching TV, playing computer games or eating sweets for a day, a couple of days, or even a week. Sometimes I'll reduce or void their pocket money for a week. In more extreme cases I'll make them go to bed thirty minutes ahead of schedule. Because I know what my kids really like to do, it isn't difficult to ban something fairly simple and still manage to get the point across.

● *Level Five ~ the ultimate combo.* I rarely have to resort to this level of discipline because, once experienced, it isn't the kind of thing a child wants to go through again. It sounds dramatic, I know, but basically it's just a multiple ban combined with a series of early nights. For example, no TV, no computer games, no pocket money and no sweets for a whole week plus they have to go to bed thirty minutes early each night for three nights. From my point of view, all of this is small stuff, but to my kids it really is a big deal.

As a great dad it's up to you to create your own 'levels' of discipline to suit the attitudes and personalities of your own kids. Once you have decided on such levels, you can objectively and calmly apply the appropriate level according to the misbehaviour in question, rather than relying on how you feel in the heat of the moment.

Principle 5: Help your child to learn something from the experience

Human beings learn their most important lessons from the mistakes they make. The sooner the lesson is learned, the less chance there is of the same mistake being repeated in the future. It is therefore in the best interests of everyone concerned that you help your child to learn something useful from every situation where disciplining is needed.

The simplest way of helping your child to learn something is simply to wait until he or she has paid the price for the misbehaviour – for example, at the end of the week if you've banned TV for several days – and ask a few questions:

- Do you remember why your behaviour was inappropriate?

- Do you understand why it was necessary for me to ban the TV for three days?

- Can I trust you to avoid misbehaving in that way in the future?

- What have you learned from this experience?

This interaction with your child will help him or her to feel respected and loved, and to see that you disciplined only because you had reason to do so.

A few final words on discipline

It is important to realise that everyone makes mistakes, and that often a small mistake needn't be disciplined, but simply pointed out. When you learned to drive a car, the instructor didn't give you a dressing down every time you crunched the gears – he just told you what you were doing wrong and how to do better next time. Often this is all that our kids need, so do exercise common sense and be patient with them before rushing into anything.

The second main thing I want to underline here is that the disciplinary measures discussed presume that your child is able to understand the relationship between actions and consequences. If your child can't understand this relationship because he is too young or because he has special needs which make understanding difficult, then you need to adjust your strategy accordingly. (Chapter 20 discusses how to be a great dad to a child with special needs.)

Finally, as I hope this chapter has shown, there are many more options available to us as parents than simply smacking our kids when they misbehave. Parents have been smacking their kids for decades, yet they still misbehave, so why even consider continuing to do something which doesn't seem to benefit anyone? I hope that the alternative strategies outlined here have encouraged you to become an enlightened great dad who disciplines his children with love, calmness and clarity, and thereby helps them to learn something positive from the experience.

Summary of Chapter 11

- Discipline is not something that we dish out in order to punish bad behaviour. It is a tool we need to use carefully and compassionately in order to teach our kids that their actions have consequences.
- Children are fairly easy to discipline as long as certain sensible principles are adhered to:
  - Principle 1: Discipline from a place of love, not anger.
  - Principle 2: Verbally identify what your child did wrong.
  - Principle 3: Explain the consequences of the poor behaviour.
  - Principle 4: Decide on the appropriate form of discipline.
  - Principle 5: Help your child to learn something from the experience.
- It is important to realise that everyone makes mistakes, and that often a small mistake needn't be disciplined, but simply pointed out.

CHAPTER 12

Money

Providing food, clothes, warmth, shelter, entertainment and education for your kids costs money, and the older your kids get, the more money it will take to provide for them. It is therefore vitally important that you learn to manage your finances properly as soon as you can. If this sounds a little dull then don't worry – the good news is that setting up an effective financial management system is something you only need to do once in any great depth. After that, all you need to do is update it from time to time to ensure that it still meets your needs. If that sounds reasonable to you, let's get started.

Where does all the money go?

The first step to managing your money effectively is to identify exactly how you are currently spending it. Most people spend money quite unconsciously as and when the need arises, and if they aren't careful they can often spend so much on luxuries that they don't have anything left over for essentials. This usually comes as something of a surprise, and the mantra among many people at the end of each month is the same: 'Where did all the money go?'

Finding the answer to this question isn't difficult, but it will require you to be diligent and honest. Here's what you need to do:

- Obtain a small notebook that you can carry around with you all day. This is what you will use as your 'money diary' for the next thirty days.

- Note down all money that is deducted automatically from your bank account each month via direct debits and standing orders, such as mortgage payments, insurance premiums, loan repayments, etc.

- Note down all money that is automatically charged to a credit card each month, such as Internet subscriptions, satellite television subscriptions, etc.

- For thirty days, every time you spend any amount of money, either in cash or using a debit or credit card, note down the date, the amount spent and the item purchased. Don't omit the small stuff here – spending money on a daily newspaper or on a sandwich at lunchtime might seem insignificant, but it all adds up, so note it down.

At the end of the thirty days, sit down with your money diary and add up all that you have spent. If you are like most people, you will be surprised by just how much you have managed to spend in a single month. You may also be surprised at how much you have spent on luxuries and non-essentials. This is all perfectly common and nothing to be concerned about. The aim of this exercise was simply to obtain an accurate answer to the question, 'Where did all the money go?'

Creating a family budget

Now that you know exactly how you are currently spending your money, you are ready to create a family budget. The word 'budget' has negative connotations for many people, because it makes them think of scrimping and saving and missing out on all the 'fun' things that they like to enjoy – but really this view of budgeting is inaccurate. When all is said and done, a budget is not a *scrimping* plan that causes discomfort or restriction. Rather, it is a *spending* plan that will enable you to take total control over your financial life and obtain a level of financial freedom that most people can't even imagine.

The first step to creating a family budget is to calculate exactly how much money you have coming in each month. For many people, this will simply be their main salary, but others may need to include additional forms of income such as state benefits, child allowance, etc. Whatever your income figure is, write it down here:

INCOME = £_____

Next, make a list of all items of expenditure that are absolutely essential. For example:

- clothes
- Council Tax
- food and groceries
- insurance premiums
- loan/hire purchase/credit card payments
- mortgage or rent payments
- petrol/car expenses
- school fees/lunch money, etc.
- telephone bills
- travel to/from work
- TV licence payments
- utility payments (for gas, electricity, water, etc.).

It is usually a good idea to note down the payments for an average month. Where monthly figures aren't available, come up with an accurate estimate by dividing the expenditure for the previous year by twelve. For example, if you spent £648 on electricity bills in the previous year, this would be listed on your monthly budget as 'Electricity = £54.00'.

When you have itemised all essential monthly expenses in this way, the next step is to total up all items on your list so that you have a final expenditure figure:

EXPENDITURE = £_____

Now here comes the interesting bit. Take your income figure and deduct your expenditure figure. The difference, which is your surplus, should be noted below:

SURPLUS = £_____

If your surplus is a negative figure, then clearly something needs to be done as you are currently spending more than you earn. In this case, I suggest that you skip the rest of this chapter and instead consult your nearest branch of the Citizens Advice Bureau. The CAB has a great deal of experience in helping people to turn this kind of situation around, so the sooner you contact them, the faster you will be able to benefit.

If you are still reading then I assume that your surplus figure is positive. This means that you have money to spare after paying for all your expenses, and for many of you it will be a larger surplus than you expected. Your job now is to consciously plan how to use that surplus so that you and your family have the most fulfilling lives possible.

A good place to begin is to think about what you really want out of life, and what you want for your children. Do you want your kids to go to university? Do you want to be able to pay for a wedding ten or twenty years down the line? Do you want a comfortable pension in place for when you retire? All of these things cost substantial amounts of money, so simply taking a happy-go-lucky approach and hoping that you'll be able to afford them when the time comes isn't a good idea.

Instead, take steps now to invest a portion of your monthly surplus in your future. The added benefit of doing this is that you bring the magic of compound interest into play. To illustrate just how beneficial compound interest can be, consider the following.

If you were to invest £1000 in an interest-bearing account that pays 4 per cent each year, and you didn't add a single penny more, in twenty years your £1000 would have grown to £2191.12. If you found an account paying 8 per cent interest each year, the final figure after twenty years would be £4660.96.

Of course, I'm not suggesting that you simply open an account and let an initial deposit just sit there for twenty years, but the above figures do show how interest, accumulated over time, can help savings grow at a phenomenal rate. In a sense, compound interest is free money, and all you have to do to collect it is plan ahead and start saving now instead of later.

There are a number of saving options available to those who have a long-term goal in mind. If you have a good knowledge of the stock-market you could invest directly in shares. If you don't have that great a knowledge, or you don't want to go that route, you could alternatively invest in an ISA, share portfolio or mutual fund.

You don't need a fortune to realise your long-term financial goals. Saving just £20 a month towards your son or daughter's university education is a lot better than making no provision at all, and as your finances improve over the years you can increase the sums invested accordingly.

When you have arranged to save a certain amount of your surplus figure towards long-term goals such as these, the rest can be used for short-term life enhancement. However, even here it can be good to plan ahead, so consider setting aside a monthly sum to cover:

- birthdays and Christmas expenses

- annual holidays

- an emergency fund.

The emergency fund is simply money on deposit that is there to help you cope with those unexpected expenses we all experience from time to time, such as having to buy a new washing machine or pay for essential car repairs. Many families don't have the foresight to make this kind of provision, but doing so – even if it's just £20 a month – will go a long way to reducing stress when the need to meet emergency expenses arises.

Whatever is left of your surplus after making all of these provisions can, you'll be glad to hear, be spent as you like on the little things that make life more enjoyable.

You should remember that all of the above principles apply no matter how large or how small your income is. If you can afford to save £100 a month for your daughter's wedding, then save £100 a month. If you can only afford to save £5 a month towards

Christmas expenses, then save just £5 a month. Good financial management is not about how much you set aside for various long-term goals and annual expenses, but more about setting something aside – period.

Once your budget has been created, all you have to do to benefit from it is use it. This might feel awkward at first, but – like any new habit – it becomes easy if you have the gumption to discipline yourself and stick with it. Do this and you can take pride in the fact that you are doing all you can to manage your finances in a responsible and sensible manner.

Teaching sound financial principles to your kids

If you were taught sound financial principles as a child, then much of what we have just discussed will be familiar to you already to some extent. As a great dad, it's now your job to help your own child develop good attitudes and habits about money. Here are the three main principles you would do well to emphasise.

Principle 1: Money is earned

The first principle we need to teach kids is that money is earned. It sounds like common sense, I know, but many kids – especially younger ones – tend to assume that we have unlimited quantities of the stuff and can therefore buy anything we like. The sooner kids realise that money comes as the result of working hard or smart, the sooner they will develop a healthy respect for it. They will also grow up knowing that if they want to make money of their own, they will need to work for it, and it won't simply be handed to them on a plate.

Principle 2: Saving is an important habit

If you had saved 10 per cent of all the money you have received in your lifetime (including pocket money as a child, monetary gifts and all your take-home earnings from every job you've ever had), how much would you have set aside right at this moment? Think about this question seriously for a moment before continuing. Use a calculator if necessary.

The chances are that you'd be fairly wealthy or, at the very least, a lot more wealthy than you are right now, especially if you'd put your 10 per cent savings in an interest-bearing account. But the chances are also that you haven't done this in actuality, and that you're now wishing that you had.

With this realisation in mind, why not encourage your child to get into the habit of saving 10 per cent of all the money he or she receives? Habits established during childhood can serve a human being well for an entire lifetime, so even though the child may only be saving a couple of pennies a week at first, the eventual benefit could be infinitely greater.

Principle 3: Budgeting is essential

The third principle you can teach as your kids get older is that of budgeting. As you have read yourself in this chapter, budgeting gives a person a great deal more control over personal finances than spending money without any real conscious forethought – and passing this knowledge on to your children is something they will certainly appreciate in the coming years.

How, you may be thinking, can children learn to budget when they don't have anything to budget for? Good question. The answer is that we need to help our kids learn the basics of budgeting, and leave the details until later. For example, a child could set a simple 'long-term' goal of being able to afford a certain £10 toy at some point in the future. A ten-year-old boy who receives pocket money of (say) £4 per week could then choose to save £1 per week until having enough to make the purchase. If he is also already in the habit of saving 10 per cent of his money for his genuinely longer term future (which would be 40p in this case), he would have £2.60 pocket money left over to enjoy as he pleased.

This is a simple approach to take, but it's still budgeting. As your child learns that the principle of budgeting works in small things, he or she will be far more likely to use it later when financial matters get more complicated.

A word on pocket money and allowances

Some parents hold the opinion that children shouldn't receive pocket money or allowances, and whilst every parent is free to have their individual opinion, I believe that pocket money is a positive thing. The simple reason for my stance is that giving kids a small amount of money for their own use helps them to develop in several important ways:

- First, receiving a fixed amount of pocket money on a regular basis helps kids understand that there isn't an infinite amount of the stuff and that they can't afford everything they want. Instead, they have to prioritise their desires and learn to give up some things so that they can afford other things.

- Second, pocket money helps kids to be more responsible. If they learn to look after their pocket money properly, they will automatically be learning to take better care of themselves.

- Third, receiving pocket money allows a child to plan ahead. The child can think about what he or she might like to have in the future and make decisions about how to obtain those goals by managing finances in a more conscious way.

Of course, kids are kids, and sometimes all they will want to do is blow every penny on a comic and bubble gum. That's to be expected from time to time. However, I believe that giving a child who is able to handle money a certain amount of pocket money each week does a lot of good, and should be seriously considered by all great dads.

SUMMARY OF CHAPTER 12

- It is vitally important that you learn to manage your finances properly as soon as you can.
- Start by obtaining a small notebook to use as a money diary and for thirty days keep a note of every penny you spend. This will enable you to answer the question: 'Where did all the money go?'
- Next, create a budget. Remember that a budget is not a scrimping plan, but a spending plan, and will enable you to get total control over your finances.
- When you have your own financial life in order, start teaching your children the three main principles we looked at:
  - Principle 1: Money is earned.
  - Principle 2: Saving is an important habit.
  - Principle 3: Budgeting is essential.

CHAPTER 13

Disagreements

Disagreements, arguments and conflicts are common in all families, no matter how good your relationships are. Sometimes the disagreements will be small and petty, as happens when a young child says 'I want an ice-cream' and the father says no. At other times the disagreements will be large, theatrical and serious, as happens when a teenager gets caught drinking underage and defends his right to do so. And, of course, disagreements can also arise between you and your partner when you have differing views on how your child should be disciplined, rewarded or spend their free time.

Because disagreements are a fact of life, it is important that you learn to deal with them effectively. This is best done by:

- understanding how and why disagreements take place

- taking steps to reduce the likelihood of disagreements

- learning to resolve disagreements that do arise, in a positive way.

How and why disagreements take place

Most people think that disagreements arise when one person who is obviously 'wrong' takes issue with another person who is obviously 'right', but this is a very adversarial way of looking at things, and not one that is conducive to finding a positive resolution.

People who hold this view often find that the cause of the disagreement tends to become less important than the idea of 'winning the battle', which is why so many arguments over relatively trifling matters can sometimes end up getting blown out of all proportion.

A far more positive way of looking at disagreements is as a conflict of opinions based on differing values. In other words, a disagreement arises when two people who have different values both try to defend their 'right' point of view. For example:

- Your child values having fun more than she values doing her homework.

- You value your child doing her homework more than you value her having fun.

In this scenario, if your daughter insists on playing a video game instead of studying, you are likely to have a disagreement – not because you are necessarily 'right' and she is 'wrong', but simply because you have differing values.

The same conflict in values can occur between partners. For example:

- Your partner values spending time with you more than she values you working.

- You value working more than you value spending time with her.

In this scenario, if you repeatedly choose to work overtime then you will probably be on course for a disagreement – not because working is 'wrong', but because it conflicts with your partner's chief value of spending time with you at home.

Human beings can be fairly patient when they want to be, so in many cases an occasional challenge to their values may well be ignored. However, if their values are challenged repeatedly then at some point they will feel the need to stand up and defend them, and this is where disagreements arise.

Understanding this definite relationship between values and disagreements is helpful because it makes us realise that resolving an argument must involve a lot more than simply proving who is 'right' and who is 'wrong'. It also gives us a clue to how we might be able to reduce the likelihood of disagreements arising in the first place.

Reducing the likelihood of disagreements

If disagreements occur because of conflicting values, it makes sense that a good way to reduce the likelihood of disagreements arising is to understand the values of the people we associate with on a daily basis. Once we know what our partner and children value, we can try to ensure that we make room for those values as well as our own.

For example, let's say that your son loves eating burgers from a local fast-food outlet. You think it's unhealthy. Instead of banning the fast-food outlet altogether (and thereby insisting that your values are more important than those of your child), you could agree to let your son have a burger once a fortnight. He may still protest a little, but is likely to be far more amenable to this idea than he would be to a total ban.

The same principle applies with your partner. If your partner values spending time with you in the evenings more than she values you working late, repeatedly doing the latter will only lead to you having a disagreement. Instead, consider alternatives that would allow you to respect her values, such as going to work an hour earlier or working through a lunch hour.

All of this works in the opposite direction too. If you make sure that your partner and kids understand the values that are important to you, the chances of them routinely acting in ways that threaten those values are greatly reduced.

Resolving disagreements in a positive way

Even if you do all that has been suggested so far, you will still have disagreements from time to time. This being the case, it is important that you learn to resolve them in a positive way. There is no 'one size fits all' magic formula, but there are six simple steps that you can use to help you resolve disagreements effectively.

Step 1: Remember that you're all on the same team

Begin by taking a few minutes out to pause and remember that you and your child and partner are all on the same team. You and your partner want what's best for your child, and your child wants the same. Whilst a disagreement arises because your idea of 'what's best' differs from that of your child, the underlying motive is identical. Proceeding with this more enlightened frame of mind will help you to avoid wanting to 'win' an argument and to instead negotiate a resolution that satisfies everyone.

Step 2: Remember the principles of good communication

I presented the seven principles of good communication in Chapter 8, so I won't repeat myself here. Suffice it to say that you need to keep those principles in mind when faced with a disagreement of any kind. In particular, remember these five principles:

- Think before you speak.

- Give them your full attention.

- Listen.

- Talk, don't preach.

- Don't expect 100 per cent agreement.

Step 3: Identify the problem

It is easy to allow our emotions to cloud the issue when disagreements arise, and this can lead to people arguing over side-issues that have nothing at all to do with the real conflict in values. You can combat this tendency by getting everyone concerned to identify the problem that they believe is at the core of the disagreement. Try to be as specific as possible when doing this, because a well-defined problem will be much easier to solve than one that is vague. Asking the following questions will help here:

- What is the central problem?

- Why is this a problem?

- Who is most affected by the problem?

When discussing the problem, make sure that you allow your child and/or partner to talk freely. Interrupting to put forward your own point of view will only frustrate people, and escalate the disagreement further.

Step 4: Identify the values threatened

Once you have clearly identified the problem at the centre of the disagreement, move on to identifying the value(s) that are threatened by this problem. If you don't know what values are being threatened, it will be difficult to resolve the disagreement in a way that satisfies everyone. However, if you do know the values, this knowledge in itself can suggest a positive way forward.

For example, if your child is arguing with you because she doesn't want to go to Brownies, you can ask why going would upset her. She might then respond that going would mean she has less time to learn her spellings for a test at school tomorrow morning, and she is worried about getting a poor score. In this case, the value that she thinks is at risk is that of doing well at school.

Step 5: Discuss all possible solutions

The next step is to start brainstorming and come up with as many ways as you can think of to solve the problem without sacrificing the value that has been identified as being threatened. Don't judge anyone's ideas at this stage, but simply focus on coming up with as many of them as possible. When everyone concerned has run out of ideas, move on to Step 6.

Step 6: Agree on a satisfactory solution

Now that you have brainstormed all possible options, it is time to agree on a satisfactory solution. A satisfactory solution is one that solves the problem without sacrificing the value that has been identified as being threatened.

For example, your daughter doesn't want to go to Brownies this week. That's the problem. She doesn't want to go because that would mean having less time to learn her spellings for a test at school tomorrow morning. Doing well at school is the value perceived as being at risk. In this case, a satisfactory solution would be one that helps everyone to agree on the Brownies issue without sacrificing the idea of doing well at school. Two examples of such a satisfactory solution might be:

- Agree that she can skip Brownies this week in order to focus on learning spellings for the school test.

- Allow her to stay up half an hour later than usual so that she can learn the spellings before going to bed.

It is important that everyone agrees to the solution, otherwise further disagreements may arise in the future when the solution is implemented. Compromise may be required on all sides, so don't think that just because you're a great dad you'll always come up with a solution that suits you more than others. The greatest dads are those who are willing to be the most flexible when that kind of approach is appropriate.

This six-step process is obviously designed for more serious disagreements, so sitting everyone down to discuss the ins and outs of your child wanting an ice-cream at two in the morning is probably not going to make your family life more harmonious. Similarly, I am not suggesting that you have to have lengthy discussions every time you find yourself having to say 'no' to your child. Use common sense here and learn to adapt the principles of the process to suit your needs as and when the situation occurs.

Dealing with sibling rivalry

If you have two or more children then sibling rivalry is something you will need to learn to deal with. It shows itself in many different ways, but the most common manifestations include whining ('Dad, Tom's being too noisy / Tom's making a mess / Tom's pulling faces at me'), name-calling ('Idiot / You're ugly and fat / You're both those things and stupid with it'), and physical aggression (snatching things from each other, hitting each other, etc.).

A small amount of sibling rivalry is perfectly natural and occurs in almost all species where multiple youngsters are raised together. However, this doesn't mean that you should allow it to become excessive or get out of control. You should take sensible steps to keep rivalry at a minimum and to deal with heated outbursts when they crop up. Here's how.

Principle 1: Treat all children equally

The most important thing you can do to prevent sibling rivalry is to make sure that you treat all of your children equally. Give each of them the same amount of love, care and attention so that nobody feels particularly favoured or neglected. This sounds obvious – and it is – but there are times when we can unwittingly give one child more attention than another. For example, parents who have a second child naturally have to focus quite a lot of attention on their newborn, and if they aren't careful their older child may begin to feel left out and therefore resent the sibling for 'robbing them' of your attention.

Principle 2: Give your children collective and individual attention

There are two extremes which parents can gravitate towards when raising two or more children. One is to always give their children collective attention, by taking all of their kids out for a meal, for example, or to play in the park together. The other extreme is to always give their children individual attention, by playing a game with one child and then playing a different game with another. Both approaches are healthy, but not to the exclusion of the other.

Ideally, you should aim to give your children a balance of both collective and individual attention. By regularly having fun together, your kids will have plenty of opportunities to get along together and form strong, happy relationships. By regularly having their own slots of 'personal time' with you in addition, they will feel loved and cared for as individuals.

Principle 3: Adopt a zero-tolerance policy for physical aggression

If you allow your children to snatch things from each other, or to hit, scratch and bite each other – regardless of the excuses they may make about provocation – you not only risk one of your kids getting seriously hurt, but you are also teaching (albeit passively) that physical aggression is acceptable. It isn't – not for you, not for your kids and not for anyone else.

Kids who are used to being physically aggressive at home are more likely to act in the same way at school. This can lead to all sorts of problems, including bullying, fights, classroom disruption and – in a worst-case scenario – expulsion.

Start as you mean to go on, and adopt a zero-tolerance policy for physical aggression. The first time one of your kids gets deliberately rough (scrapes accidentally received during the normal rough and tumble of play are obviously a different matter entirely) give a verbal warning and explain why physical aggression isn't acceptable. Then, if he or she repeats the behaviour, raise the discipline level a notch to drive the point home.

Principle 4: When a spat breaks out, promote communication

When non-physical disagreements occur between siblings, teach your kids to resolve their difficulties by communicating politely and honestly. Draw from the principles of good communication you read about in Chapter 8 and the six-step resolution process outlined earlier in this chapter. As you do this, try to remain objective and to be a facilitator of the communication process rather than someone who has all the answers. An important part of growing up is learning to settle disputes peacefully, so if you barge in and tell both kids what to do, they are missing out on a good opportunity to develop themselves in this area.

In most cases, sibling rivalry is nothing to be overly concerned about. Many adult siblings are just as competitive as they were when they were kids, even if they have a great relationship in every other respect. Your job as a great dad is not, therefore, to completely eradicate this natural instinct (which is virtually impossible) but to try to ensure that it is dealt with in a peaceful and fairly amicable manner.

SUMMARY OF CHAPTER 13

- Disagreements, arguments and conflicts are common in all families, no matter how good your relationships are. Because disagreements are a fact of life, it is important that you learn to deal with them effectively.

- There are six simple steps that you can use to help you resolve disagreements effectively:

  - Step 1: Remember that you're all on the same team.
  - Step 2: Remember the principles of good communication.
  - Step 3: Identify the problem.
  - Step 4: Identify the values threatened.
  - Step 5: Discuss all possible solutions.
  - Step 6: Agree on a satisfactory solution.

- A small amount of sibling rivalry is perfectly natural and occurs in almost all species where multiple youngsters are raised together. However, you should follow these principles to keep rivalry at a minimum and to deal with heated outbursts when they crop up:

  - Principle 1: Treat all children equally.
  - Principle 2: Give your children collective and individual attention.
  - Principle 3: Adopt a zero-tolerance policy for physical aggression.
  - Principle 4: When a spat breaks out, promote communication.

CHAPTER 14

Sexuality

From a kid's point of view

I'm getting a bit annoyed with my dad. The other night we were watching The Simpsons *on television and Homer kept on telling Marge that he wanted to have sex with her. I've heard some of the older boys talking a bit about sex at school, but I really haven't got a clue what they're on about, so when Homer kept on saying this, I thought I might as well ask dad.*

'What exactly is sex?' I asked him. He was eating a biscuit at the time and nearly choked. Crumbs went everywhere.

'Why do you ask?'

'Because I'm interested.'

He looked at me for a long time, clearly thinking about something, but not saying what it was. Then he asked, 'How old are you again?'

'You know how old I am!' I said. 'I'm ten!'

He nodded carefully. 'Well ask me again when you're eleven.'

Then he turned over the channel to watch the news and went back to eating the rest of his biscuit. Not only did I not find out what sex is, but I also ended up missing the rest of The Simpsons. *I never did find out if Homer got what he wanted.*

Tough questions

There are a few things in life that can make a man freeze on the spot. Having your mind go blank during an important business presentation is one of them. Getting pulled over by a traffic cop for a routine vehicle check is another. But perhaps the most daunting for most men is having their child approach them with questions related to the subject of sexuality.

Although talking about this topic with your child may not be something that feels comfortable, it is nevertheless essential. The only alternative is to remain silent on the subject, brushing aside questions repeatedly until the child stops asking them. Unfortunately, this approach almost always leads kids to get their answers from far more dubious sources – most often from their friends – and the potential risks incurred by them taking false information as fact are numerous. Underage sex is far more common among the sexually misinformed than it is among those who have a factual and balanced understanding of the subject, as are sexually transmitted diseases and pregnancies. The price a dad pays for saving his own embarrassment can therefore be substantial.

As a great dad, you will probably agree that remaining silent is not an option. So how exactly should we go about providing the sex education our kids need? How much do kids really need to know? When do they need to know it? And how do we talk about sex in such a way that we don't make it sound incredibly appealing? These are all tough questions, so let's address each of them in turn and, in doing so, come up with a sensible strategy to educate our kids in a way that genuinely benefits them.

How should you provide sex education?

The traditional way for parents to educate kids about sex was to sit them down, talk for half an hour about birds, eggs, bees, pollination (being as vague as possible and carefully avoiding bringing human beings into the conversation) before sending them on their way to figure out what the hell all that has to do with the subject. Unfortunately, I'm only half joking here. Although in previous generations parents have occasionally conceded to present 'the facts' about sex to their kids, they have often done so in a deliberately vague manner – being careful to use technical (preferably Latin) physiological terminology which, they hope, Johnny won't truly understand. This generally made parents feel better about themselves, proud that they had 'done their bit', but it didn't really provide the kind of real-world information that Johnny wanted, and needed, to know.

Today we are a lot more enlightened, and although a relaxed chat about the topic is still the main weapon in our battle against misinformation, we do have one other important resource available that can make this conversation a great deal easier to deal with. This resource is books.

There are many books that have been written specifically for children dealing with a wide range of subjects, including puberty, periods, hormones, intercourse, homosexual lifestyles and sexually transmitted diseases. One of the best books available is *Let's Talk About Sex,* written by Robie H. Harris and illustrated by Michael Emberley. This book is aimed at kids preparing for and going through puberty, and presents all the factual information they need in a language they can relate to. Endorsed by fpa (formerly known as the Family Planning Association), *Let's Talk About Sex* is a book I would personally recommend all great dads to obtain when the time is right. The advantages of giving an age-appropriate sex education book to a child are numerous:

- By giving him or her a book on the topic, you are demonstrating that you aren't embarrassed by it. This will make you seem more approachable if your child has a question that isn't covered.

- You are providing your child with a reliable source of information that he or she can refer to again and again. This is important because it reduces the likelihood of your child relying on misinformation from friends.

- As your child goes through physiological changes, he or she will be able to look up anything without feeling embarrassed.

None of this means that you are 'off the hook' by any means. Your child will still come to you with questions from time to time, and it will still be necessary to have a fairly detailed conversation at some point to ensure his or her understanding of the subject. But a well-chosen book can certainly make your job of educating your child a great deal easier.

What do kids need to know, and when?

There is a difference between the information a child needs to know and the information he or she would *like* to know. Children are curious creatures, and it is therefore unsurprising that most of them would like to know as much as possible about sex in as much detail as you can handle. But this isn't necessarily what they need to know, and giving too much information too soon can be just as problematic later on as giving too little information too late.

A good rule of thumb is to provide enough accurate information for your children to be able to make sound decisions and live their lives without fear or confusion. Here are some general guidelines you may find useful.

Ages 0 to 5

Kids in this age range actually need to know very little about sex. The most curious five-year-old may point at you in the bathroom and ask 'What's that?', but at this stage you can simply name the part, 'It's called a penis,' and leave it at that.

Ages 6 to 10

Kids in this age range will start asking questions. At first, the questions will probably be fairly basic and crop up when they see something on television or when they hear older kids talking in the playground at school. You can deal with most of these basic questions in a fairly casual way. For example, in response to 'Where are the nuts, because Jimmy says the football hit him in the nuts?' you could answer that 'Some people use the word nuts when they're talking about their testicles.'

Up to the age of nine or so, it's often a good idea to work with the school when fielding questions about sex. Teachers are generally very happy to help you work through this potentially difficult area of parenting, and will often be able to give you an insight into what your kids are learning about sex at school, if anything.

Later, as your child approaches puberty, you will need to be more forthcoming. If you aren't, then your child may become confused or even scared when the inevitable physiological changes associated with this time take place. At this stage, it's a good idea to sit down with your child and discuss how the body can be expected to change over the coming years, and to assure the child that you are available to answer any and all questions without embarrassment.

Ages 11 to 15

This is where your child will have plenty of questions about sexuality, so it's important to start as you mean to go on. If you haven't already done so, as soon as the questions start coming, consider buying a book specifically aimed at children on the topic of sexuality, as discussed earlier. Not only will this answer many questions directly, but it may also encourage a reluctant reader to pick up a book from time to time.

When answering questions in this age range, don't underestimate how much your child needs to know. You may think that your twelve-year-old is several years away from the possibility of having sex, but it's better to be safe than sorry. If questions about contraception and so on arise, do your best to answer them as fully as you can.

Most secondary schools have sex education programmes which use multimedia resources (videos, DVDs, etc.) to provide information on a wide range of issues such as contraception, sexually transmitted diseases, pregnancy, homosexuality and so on. Whilst parents are usually given the option of excluding their children from these sessions, it is probably unwise to exercise this option unless you have an extremely good reason for doing so.

Ages 16 to 20

At some point during this stage of their lives, kids will begin taking their theoretical knowledge and putting it to practical use. Your role here is to provide information as and when you are asked for it, and to do so without holding anything back. If your child has a question you cannot answer, a good back-up is to refer him or her to a sexual advice centre such as the fpa. Or, alternatively, stock up with leaflets on a variety of subjects yourself so that you have something you can fall back on when the need occurs.

Talking about sex without making it incredibly appealing

Let's face it, sex is exciting, and we know it. So how can we talk about this subject without making it sound incredibly appealing to a ten- or eleven-year-old? There are a number of guidelines we can follow in this respect:

- Make sure your child knows the legal age of consent from the outset. Tell the child that it's against the law to have sex under the age of sixteen, and that this law is in place for a very good reason – underage sex can lead to a number of very serious problems.

- Talk about these serious problems openly. Tell your child about the dangers of sexually transmitted disease, the AIDS virus and pregnancy. By making it clear that sex can cause physical illness when it is experienced without proper preparation, your child will be less likely to experiment.

- Talk about sex in the context of committed relationships. Younger kids tend to display an interest in sex long before they display any interest in relationships, so by presenting one in the context of the other you will lessen the appeal.

- Don't talk about sex constantly. Although educating your children is essential, it is better to let them learn gradually as they grow up, rather than to hit them with a mass of information all at once. By taking this approach, your kids will view sex as just another part of life, and not the 'be all and end all' of adulthood.

Dealing with boyfriends and girlfriends

At some point, your child will discover the appeal of forming close personal relationships and a boyfriend or girlfriend will appear on the scene. Initially, the term 'boyfriend' or 'girlfriend' will be used very loosely, so don't panic when your ten-year-old starts using it at the dinner table. As your kids get older, however, their relationships will become more serious, and could well involve kissing and cuddling by the time they reach the age of fourteen or fifteen. At this stage you will need to tread the fine line between allowing your child the freedom to learn about relationships in this way, and setting sensible boundaries to protect them. You also need to do what you can to help your child learn something from the relationship. The following ideas will help you in this area:

- Keep the child's bedroom door open. Some parents choose to keep their kids' rooms out of bounds as far as members of the opposite sex are concerned, and this is a valid option. However, if you do allow use of the bedroom it is a good idea to keep the door open at all times so that the kids aren't able to abuse their privacy.

- Educate your child about relationships. Make him or her aware of what is and what is not acceptable behaviour in a relationship; and unless your kid is over sixteen, your stance should be that sexual activity is not acceptable.

- Encourage your child to maintain friendships with others. Sometimes a child will neglect other friends in order to focus on the boyfriend or girlfriend. Unfortunately when the relationship breaks down, this could leave your child without the support of peers.

- Don't mock the relationship. To you it's puppy love and you know it won't last. But to your child, it's the real thing and destined to last a lifetime. Don't allow your more objective opinion to negate the relationship for your child. Instead, allow the child to enjoy it and learn from it by taking it more seriously.

- Set curfews, rules and boundaries so that you know exactly where your child is at all times. Your child is always your own responsibility, not the responsibility of the boyfriend or girlfriend. No matter how trustworthy they seem, remember this.

- Be ready to pick up the pieces. When the relationship ends, your child may be upset. This is perfectly natural and enables your child to learn that relationships aren't all positive. Be supportive after a break-up and do what you can to give your child something else to focus on until time heals the wounds.

Summary of Chapter 14

- Although talking about sexuality with your child may not be something that feels comfortable, it is nevertheless essential. A relaxed chat about the topic is still the main weapon in our battle against misinformation, so don't be afraid to talk honestly and openly about sex when the time is right.

- As well as talking, you can give your child one of the many books on sex written specifically for their age group. The title I most strongly recommend for kids preparing for and going through puberty is *Let's Talk About Sex,* written by Robie H. Harris and illustrated by Michael Emberley.

- There is a difference between the information a child needs to know and the information the child would like to know. A good rule of thumb is to provide enough accurate information for your child to be able to make sound decisions and live his or her life without fear or confusion.

- You can talk about sex without making it sound overly appealing:
  - Make sure that your child knows the legal age of consent from the outset.
  - Talk about the problems associated with underage and unprotected sex.
  - Talk about sex in the context of committed relationships.
  - Allow your child to learn gradually as he or she grows up.

CHAPTER 15

Encouraging an Empowering World View

From a kid's point of view

I'm fifteen years old, working hard so that I get good exam results next year, and all of a sudden it occurs to me – what's the point? What's the point of getting good results, of going on to further education, of getting a good job? I mean, we all die eventually, don't we? And the way the world's going, we might have wiped ourselves out before I even get to that point.

I know lots of people who left school with plenty of good grades and their heads full of big ideas. All of them are either on the dole or working in dead-end jobs that they hate. So I'm thinking, why bother making plans in the first place? Why not just enjoy life as it comes? Why not just focus on having one big party until the Reaper Man gets me?

What's the point?

At some point during adolescence, most kids start to ask questions about their lives and the world they live in. Some kids find answers that empower them and drive them forward to strive for lives of happiness and success. But others don't, and these either struggle with a very real sense of depression or look for a sense of purpose by joining any one of a number of groups that are able to provide them with a greater vision of themselves.

Unfortunately, there are some groups – commonly known as cults – that make a deliberate effort to market themselves to young people who are shopping for a purpose in life. The only way to protect your child from such organisations is to help your child develop his or her own sense of purpose.

In previous generations, kids got a sense of what life is all about from formal institutions such as the church or from the example of tradition. However, in recent decades, many of these institutions and traditions have lost their power to influence, and the result is an increasing number of kids who lack direction. And who can blame them? Morality, ethics and integrity are all words that have lost their edge in the modern world, and the only 'universal truth' still promoted widely is that people should make up their own 'truths' as they go along.

All of this sounds rather theoretical, I know, but the subject of how we view ourselves and the world is in fact incredibly practical, because it shapes who we become as human beings. The view your children have of the world – and of their place in it – will have a dramatic impact on how they live their lives. It will determine the goals they aspire to, the way they interact with other people, the way they work, the way they spend their free time, the way they speak and the way they conduct themselves.

Nine viewpoints on life

Because it is so important, your job as a great dad is to encourage a world view that will empower your kids to reach their full potential and help them to avoid a number of common mistakes at the same time. The best way to do this is not by preaching empty words, but by adopting a more positive world view yourself and living this on a daily basis, thereby teaching by example. Here are the main attitudes, beliefs and principles which you should consider adopting for this purpose:

Viewpoint 1: The world is a benevolent place

People who view the world as an intrinsically dangerous and oppressive place tend to live life at arm's length. They are afraid to take even sensible risks and are constantly looking for the negative things in life to 'prove' their belief that the world is out to get them. Naturally, this kind of attitude doesn't empower individuals to enjoy life to the full, but rather encourages them to hide themselves away in an effort to keep as low a profile as possible.

Other people who view the world as an essentially friendly and benevolent place tend to live their lives with enthusiasm. They are willing to take sensible risks because they know that, in a worst-case scenario, they will be able to pick themselves up and start over again. This ability to take more risks in life generally means that they experience more happiness and success than other people. Of course, they experience more sadness and let-downs as well; but because people with this attitude are constantly looking for the positive things in life to 'prove' that the world is fundamentally kind to them, these more negative experiences are often ignored, or at the very least forgotten rather quickly.

It goes without saying that the world can be a dangerous place from time to time, but unfortunately it's the only one we have. We can't simply pack our things and move to a new one, so our only choice is to embrace where we are or to spend our lives hiding from it. Choosing to believe that the world is a benevolent place in which negative things happen from time to time is much more empowering than choosing to believe the opposite.

Viewpoint 2: Self-belief is essential

In some quarters, people who believe in themselves are considered arrogant, egotistical and full of themselves. This is a shame, because people who believe in themselves tend to have much happier lives than those who don't. Of course, this doesn't mean that we should adopt the attitude that we are intrinsically superior to other people, but neither should we believe that we are intrinsically inferior to them.

If we don't believe in ourselves, how can we expect other people to believe in us? If we don't value ourselves as being attractive in our own unique ways, how can we expect others to find us attractive? If we don't say that we can do a certain thing, who in his right mind will ever give us the chance to prove it? Believing in ourselves is not a sin, but a prerequisite to living a happy and productive life. It is self-belief that enables individuals with backgrounds of poverty and misery to become wealthy and successful, rather than settling for more of the same. It is self-belief that enables the physically disadvantaged to make the most of what they have, rather than to sit wallowing in self-pity. And it is self-belief that will empower our kids to make the most of their lives, rather than being willing to settle for, as Thoreau put it, lives of quiet desperation.

Viewpoint 3: We are what we think

What we believe about ourselves as individuals determines what we will try and what we will avoid. It also greatly influences how other people perceive us to be. An entrepreneur who believes that his product is the best on earth will tend to become far more successful than one who believes that his product is mediocre. A person who believes himself to be attractive will tend to be more popular among others than a person who believes himself to be ugly.

As great dads, we need to encourage our kids to see themselves in a positive way. We need to teach them to 'accentuate the positive' and 'eliminate the negative' so that they create a self-image that is strong, confident and resourceful.

Viewpoint 4: Happiness is a choice

Many people spend their whole lives chasing happiness in the mistaken belief that it is a commodity that somehow needs to be sought and obtained. Some look for it at the very top of the career ladder. Others think that it can be gained by accumulating a lot of money. Still others try to find it through sex or drugs. Unfortunately, as anyone who has tried these things will freely admit, happiness is not to be found in any of these places.

Happiness is not something that is obtained, but something that all of us can choose to experience whenever we want to. It is true that having a nice house and a nice car may make it easier to choose happiness, but these things are by no means prerequisites, and they certainly don't guarantee the condition.

That's why there are so many externally comfortable people who aren't happy and why there are also plenty of people who are deeply happy despite some extremely challenging personal circumstances.

How does an individual choose to be happy? By simply choosing! In the bigger scheme of things, every day lived above ground is really a great day, so why not choose to be happy as soon as you wake up in the morning? By adopting this habit, you can be happy no matter what life throws at you – and because you are happy, you will deal with life a lot more effectively than someone who chooses to be frustrated or sad, and you'll set a great example.

Viewpoint 5: Success is achievable

The people who succeed in life through their own efforts (which automatically discounts all lottery winners and the like) tend to be those who believe that success is achievable. This is to be expected. If a person doesn't believe that success is really achievable, then what's the point of even trying? He or she might as well switch on the TV and watch soap operas instead.

Contrary to what most people believe, success is not dependent on class, race, age, background, financial backing or any other such factor. Evidence for this observation can be found in the Biography section of your local library. There you will read stories of people who, born with almost every disadvantage under the sun, went beyond the expectations of their peers to achieve extremely high levels of success. This age-old 'rags to riches' story isn't to be found only in the world of movie stars and media celebrities, but also in every other arena of life, including politics, sport, art and literature.

If so many people with such disadvantaged origins have dared to believe that success is achievable, and proven the assumption by making it happen, it makes sense that we should all dare to believe the same. Start by believing it yourself, then live this belief and encourage your children to follow suit.

Viewpoint 6: Productive work is always rewarded

Despite the fact that the buzz-words of the twenty-first century tend to be ones like 'instant', 'easy' and 'effortless', the reality of life is that people who commit themselves to working productively feel far better about themselves than those who are always looking to take the lazy option. Productive work is always rewarded. This doesn't mean that there is always a financial reward, but working hard isn't just about making money. The real value in hard work is in the way it helps us to develop character, self-discipline and a sense of fulfilment.

Encouraging our kids to enjoy working productively for its own sake is something that will enable them to reap benefits for the rest of their lives, especially in career terms. Fashions and fads come and go, but those who work productively and enjoy doing so are always recognised for their immense value to society.

Viewpoint 7: Setting goals is important

Unless we have a very clear idea of where we want to go in life, how can we ever expect to get there, and how will we know when we've arrived? Human beings are goal-oriented creatures, and we feel most fulfilled when we are pursuing a target that we have set for ourselves. But if we don't set goals, life can begin to feel directionless, and even dull.

It isn't difficult to encourage our children to set goals. They can set goals related to their hobbies and interests, or ones related to their homework schedules. The nature of their goals isn't nearly as important as establishing the habit of setting them. However, we do need to ensure that our kids have a realistic chance of achieving their goals, otherwise they will soon get frustrated and lose interest.

Goals should be set down in writing so that they can be referred to on a regular basis. Writing down goals also makes it possible for a child to cross them out as they are achieved, and therefore gives them a very real sense of accomplishment.

Viewpoint 8: Tough times come along to help us grow

Whether it's doing badly on an examination, breaking up with a partner, losing a job we enjoy or struggling with ill-health, we all face tough times in life. There is no use bringing our kids up to believe otherwise. Instead, we need to give them a way to view such tough times in a positive and empowering way so that they don't feel overwhelmed by them.

One good way of encouraging an empowering stance is to view tough times as things that help us grow. We can observe in nature that the strongest trees are often those that are exposed to the strongest winds. We can also observe that the strongest animals tend to be those with the most ferocious enemies. If we apply these observations to life as a human being, we can conclude that the tough times we face are, potentially at least, vehicles that can help us to grow and evolve in a variety of ways. This point of view won't necessarily make the tough times any less severe, but it will help us to look for the silver linings in the clouds that pass over our lives. It has been said by someone much wiser than myself that every problem we face contains the seed of an even greater benefit. By focusing on looking for the benefit, rather than on the negative side of the problem, we gain a wider perspective and can choose to take something positive from our experience.

Viewpoint 9: There are no failures, only experiences

Labelling oneself as a failure isn't empowering by any stretch of the imagination, but people do this all the time. As a result, these same people dread taking chances because they dread the thought of failing, so they choose instead to settle for lives of mediocrity rather than pursuing their full potential.

A much more empowering view to take is to say that there are no failures in life – only experiences that are there for us to learn from. Scientists don't try one thing and then, finding it doesn't work, throw the towel in because they have failed. Instead, they learn from the poor or unexpected result and adjust their approach for their next experiment. By taking this more positive attitude, each 'failed' experiment helps them to move forward until eventual success is achieved as the natural result.

It will probably serve you well to delete the word 'failure' from your vocabulary, and it should certainly not be a word you use to describe people. In my opinion, the only failures in life are those who choose not to try anything in the first place.

Adopting these nine attitudes and beliefs yourself, and then teaching them to your kids, will help to ensure that your children grow up with an empowering world view. This positive perspective will enrich all that they do, increase their chances of being happy and successful, and even make the tough times more tolerable. If that isn't empowering, I don't know what is.

SUMMARY OF CHAPTER 15

- At some point during adolescence, most kids start to ask questions about their lives and the world they live in. Your job as a great dad is to encourage a world view that will empower your kids to reach their full potential and help them to avoid a number of common mistakes.
- The best way to do this is to adopt a more positive world view yourself and to live this on a daily basis, thereby teaching by example. The main viewpoints – attitudes, beliefs and principles – you should consider adopting are:
  - Viewpoint 1: The world is a benevolent place.
  - Viewpoint 2: Self-belief is essential.
  - Viewpoint 3: We are what we think.
  - Viewpoint 4: Happiness is a choice.
  - Viewpoint 5: Success is achievable.
  - Viewpoint 6: Productive work is always rewarded.
  - Viewpoint 7: Setting goals is important.
  - Viewpoint 8: Tough times come along to help us grow.
  - Viewpoint 9: There are no failures, only experiences.

Being a Great Dad to an Adult

From an adult's point of view

Well, that's the hard part over. My first three months on the new job over and done with. It wasn't as daunting as I thought it might be, but I'm glad I paid attention at university because I'll really need to know my stuff if I'm going to achieve my career goals in the next few years.

I spoke to dad on the phone yesterday, and he asked how things had gone. I told him everything had been fine, though I had one not so good day when I had to give a verbal warning to the shop floor supervisor. I didn't like doing that very much.

'So why did you do it?' dad asked. 'He's probably been there for years. He doesn't want some kid straight out of school telling him how to do his job.'

I know my dad didn't mean any harm, but it's beginning to bug me the way he still insists on thinking of me as a kid. I was hired to do the job I do because I studied hard and got the best results in the district. I've been trained by the company and it's my responsibility to make sure that everything runs smoothly. I can't fail to live up to that responsibility just because I'm in my early twenties.

I'm no longer a twelve-year-old playing a board game. I've grown. I've matured. I'm a man now. Hopefully my dad will come to see that one day.

Letting go

Being a great dad to an adult is not always easy. Because our experience of our kids begins with them as newborns, we quickly proceed with the understanding that they are totally reliant on us for their well-being. Although kids naturally become more capable and independent as they get older, it is difficult for many fathers to get used to this. Even when their children become legal adults, parents can still find it extremely difficult to let go of the notion that their kids need them in order to survive and thrive. Instead, they unconsciously cling to the notion that, without their continual guidance, their kids would mess up their lives.

Whilst this notion might make the parents feel good about themselves (because it makes them feel needed), it isn't usually one that helps them to develop healthy adult relationships with their kids, for a couple of reasons.

First, if fathers fail to recognise that their adult kids really are adults, they will automatically assume that they need to provide continued help and guidance on a regular basis. Unfortunately, what is meant to be helpful from the fathers' point of view is often perceived as interfering by the kids, and this can cause relationships to become strained over time.

Some might think that this desire to interfere is something that parents naturally 'grow out of' as their kids get older, but in certain cases this doesn't happen. This is why there are so many people in their forties who complain that their parents still treat them like children by offering uninvited advice at every opportunity, or in some cases actually telling them what to do.

Another common drawback for parents who don't let go of their adult kids is that they usually have a tough time feeling fulfilled, because they think that their kids should still play a central role in their lives on a daily basis. When that doesn't happen (because the kids are obviously elsewhere living lives of their own) these parents tend to feel empty inside, and will continue to do so until they move on to the next phase by letting go.

Of course, it's not just fathers failing to let go that can cause problems in relationships with adult kids. Many adult kids themselves are also failing to let go. This is not because they aren't ready to live their own lives, but simply because continuing to live with their parents is a whole lot easier than being fully responsible. There is no mortgage to pay, no Council Tax to pay, meals are prepared without any effort, dirty laundry magically cleans and irons itself ... the advantages of kids remaining with parents during adulthood aren't difficult to identify. This is why an increasing number of adults are still living with their parents even in their late twenties and early thirties.

Obviously, we must be flexible with our adult kids, and I am not suggesting for a moment that we should simply throw them out on the street to fend for themselves at the age of eighteen or twenty-one. What I am suggesting is that we need to be aware of the fact that being a great dad to an adult is, in some respects, a whole different ball-game to being a great dad to a child. If we don't make this distinction then the chances are that both parents and kids will suffer as a result.

Strategies for 'second-phase' parenting

Making this important distinction would be a lot easier if we were to think of parenting our kids in terms of two separate phases. The 'first phase' would run from the birth of our kids to the age of eighteen. The 'second phase' would begin at age eighteen, when our kids legally become adults, and continue for the rest of their lives.

Looking at things in this context, it makes sense that we need different strategies for parenting in the second phase than we do for the first phase. We don't need a lot of these strategies (because if we are able to let go then our direct involvement in the lives of our adult children obviously decreases as time passes) – but we do need a few principles that we can adhere to in order to make second-phase parenting easier and more effective.

Perhaps the best way to discuss these strategies is to look at how our kids' lives will tend to change as they get older. Once we have identified the kind of things they will go through, we can suggest ways of offering various kinds of parenting support that will be both relevant and effective without being intrusive.

Ages 18 to 29

The first decade or so of adulthood is generally the most difficult for all concerned, because it is one of adjustment for both parents and kids. In this stage of life, your child will be exploring himself or herself and the world, as well as making a number of important decisions that could affect his or her future decades quite dramatically. Your child will have to choose the career to pursue, the location to live in, the hobbies and interests to develop, and so on.

For you as a great dad, this is the stage where you have to learn to let go and allow your offspring to live their lives on their own terms. You will have already spent eighteen years teaching them all that you know by walking your talk and setting a good example, so it's now up to them how they continue. The main principles you can follow here are as follows:

- Don't expect your kids to make decisions that you will always approve of. Because each adult is an individual, they will invariably choose to do things that you don't agree with. Expect this from the outset, and remember that they are fully entitled to do whatever they want to do with their lives. Their decision to adopt different beliefs and values doesn't necessarily mean that they don't love you or that they don't respect your perspective, but simply that they feel independent and confident enough to go their own way.

- Don't offer advice unless you are specifically invited to do so, and certainly don't lecture your kids on their chosen lifestyles or habits just because you personally prefer something different. Continually giving unwanted advice will eventually make your kids view you as a nag, and this can only lead to resentment.

- Be unshockable. Just as you have undoubtedly said and done things that might have shocked your own parents, so your own kids will probably take things a notch further. This is simply evolution at work. As the years pass, things change. Words that were considered obscene twenty years ago are now considered a part of normal daily vocabulary. Things that you currently think of as taboo or blasphemous may be commonplace twenty years down the line. If you accept that things change, that horizons are broadened and that your kids belong to the current generation who will push existing boundaries forward, you are less likely to be perturbed or shocked when this fact of life makes itself obvious.

- If you are asked to give advice, do so, but don't expect it to be taken. Adult kids ask for advice because they want an extra viewpoint. They want to know what you would do in a certain situation. Whilst these new perspectives may well help them to reach their own decisions, they probably won't follow your advice to the letter.

- Be encouraging. Respect the individuality of your kids and encourage them to live their lives to the full. What your kids need at this stage, more than anything else, is the knowledge that you are always there for them, and that – despite any differences you both have – you are both playing for the same team.

- Take your own life forward. When your kids reach adulthood, you as a parent have the opportunity to bring your focus back to your own life. Seize this opportunity with both hands. Take up a new hobby, spend more time travelling, and don't feel guilty about putting yourself first.

Ages 30 to 39

The second decade of adulthood is one where most people settle down for the long haul. They will focus on developing their careers, and many will get married and have kids of their own. For you as a great dad, this obviously means that you may face the prospect of becoming a grandfather at the same time. The main principles to bear in mind throughout this stage are as follows:

- Remember that your kids have their own rules. In the previous decade, your kids will have made some fairly important decisions about how they want to live, and by now those personal positions will have strengthened to the point where they are quite solid. As a great dad, respect the rules and attitudes of your kids, and don't make the common mistake of expecting them to accommodate your own rules or preferences. A good rule of thumb is to view yourself as a guest when interacting with your kids, and to show them the same level of courtesy you would show to any other host.

- Offer practical help. As you will know yourself by the time you reach this stage, having a family is not always easy, and your kids may appreciate any practical offer you make to baby-sit, etc. In most cases, your grandchildren will appreciate your involvement even more, so don't be afraid of offering practical help if you'd like to do so.

- Be circumspect with your advice. Continue to guard against giving advice when it hasn't been invited.

Ages 40 +

Once your kids reach the age of 40, they may begin taking a more philosophical approach to life. Subjects that they might not have thought about very much in the past (such as ageing, death, the meaning of life, etc.) will tend to be considered more fully, so don't be surprised if they turn to you for your opinion on these matters. Others may experience what is commonly referred to as a 'mid-life crisis', and spend time reassessing both their priorities and their lives as a whole. All of this means that the best strategies to adopt are as follows:

- Share your experience. It is a good idea to talk to your kids about your life, your beliefs and why you have lived the way you have. We're not talking about giving advice here, but simply sharing your experience so that you give your kids the opportunity of really understanding who you are as a person. At this stage, your kids will be ready to admit that they aren't as dissimilar to you as they may previously have believed.

- Listen without judging. If your kids approach you to talk about their own lives and any difficulties they are encountering, be ready to listen to them without advising or judging. If your kids do ask you for advice, aim to provide an insight into the long-term perspective you will have undoubtedly gained by this point.

- Don't be afraid of asking for help. At this time in your life, the tables may turn and you could find yourself in a position where you need help or advice yourself. If this happens, you will usually find that your kids will be more than happy to assist you, but they aren't mind-readers, so don't expect them to offer help out of the blue. Instead, speak up and explain the situation so that your kids have a chance to respond appropriately.

These strategies for second-phase parenting are not difficult to apply, but they will help you to enjoy smooth relationships with your kids throughout their adult lives. Of course, there are many other principles we have already discussed – such as communicating effectively – that apply just as much to adult children as to infants, so do be sure to continue to use any that are appropriate.

SUMMARY OF CHAPTER 16

- Being a great dad to an adult is not always easy. Being a great dad to an adult is, in some respects, a whole different ball-game to being a great dad to a child.

- It is a good idea to think of parenting in terms of two separate phases. The first phase would run from the birth of our kids to the age of eighteen. The second phase would begin at age eighteen and continue for the rest of their lives.

- There are strategies we can employ at different stages of this second phase, but the most important ones are as follows:
  - Don't expect your kids to make decisions that you will always approve of.
  - Don't offer advice unless you are specifically invited to do so.
  - Be unshockable.
  - Be encouraging.
  - Take your own life forward.

CHAPTER 17

Let's Talk About You

From a typical dad's point of view

I love my partner and my kids more than anything in the world, but sometimes ... just sometimes, I feel as if something's missing, and I don't know what it is. I have a good career, I enjoy an average salary and my family life is great, so what's my problem?

That's the question I just can't seem to answer, but I know there's a problem, for sure. On some days everything feels fine, but on others I tend to get stressed and irritable for no good reason. At these times, I just want to withdraw from everything and everyone, but obviously that's not possible for a family guy. I guess I'll just have to learn to live with it.

Just suppose ...

What would happen if:

- the world heavyweight boxing champion spent every waking hour in the ring with a variety of opponents who were all determined to keep him on the defensive?

- the Premier League champions decided to play four full 90-minute matches (plus injury time) every day of the week?

- a marathon runner reached the finishing line and then immediately set out to run an additional twenty-six miles?

- your boss forced you to work sixteen hours a day, without ever having a day off?

These questions might seem ludicrous, but that's only because you already know the answers to all of them. In each case, the results would be a dramatic loss of efficiency, an increase in physical, mental and emotional fatigue, and eventual burnout.

Being a great dad is much the same. If every moment of your day is spent giving to others – to your partner, to your boss at work, and to your kids at home – you will eventually discover that you will lose several very important things in the process, including your patience, your effectiveness and your identity as a man. At that point, you will trundle through life in a state of exhaustion, never thinking of yourself as anything other than a dad, a husband and an employee ... and wondering why the hell you don't feel as good as you used to.

Four principles to avoid burnout

Serious athletes know that if they want to reach their full potential they have to take sufficient time out of training to rest and recuperate. They don't take time out because they don't love the thrill of competing, but rather because they love it so much that they want to compete to the very best of their ability.

The same principle applies to you. If you want to be a truly great dad, if you want to be a great partner and lover, and if you want to be an effective employee at work, you need to make sure that you pay attention to your own needs as well. Here are several simple ways to do just that.

Principle 1: Make time for yourself

We considered time management principles back in Chapter 6, so you are already aware of how it is possible to make time for virtually anything in life if you have a good enough reason for doing so. What you may not have been aware of is that taking time out just for youself is not only important, it's actually essential if you are to function properly.

No matter who you are, and no matter how you view yourself, all men feel better about their lives if they recognise and honour their natural desire to withdraw from others on a regular basis. Exactly how they withdraw, and where they withdraw to, are of secondary importance. Some men like to tinker about in a garden shed. Others like to wash and wax their cars. Still others like to play a musical instrument, paint, go sailing, play golf or fly light aeroplanes.

These things may seem rather frivolous, but they all provide a man with ways to withdraw from others and enjoy relative solitude. This gives us the time and space we all need to think about our lives and our problems and to come up with strategies and game-plans to make our lives more enjoyable and effective in the future.

How much time a man needs to make for himself varies from individual to individual. Some men like to have half an hour a day to themselves. Other prefer a block of three or four hours each weekend. You should feel free to adopt whichever strategy you want to in this respect, but aim to make time for yourself on at least a weekly basis.

Principle 2: Increase your physical energy levels

The more physical energy and vitality you have available, the more effective you will be in all areas of your life. Although many people believe that the amount of physical energy they have is something they cannot control, they are generally mistaken. We can all increase our physical energy levels by adopting four simple habits.

Deep breathing

Oxygen is essential for our physical well-being. The more oxygen we have in our bodies, the more effectively it will operate. Unfortunately most people don't have good breathing habits. Instead of taking full, deep breaths that energise the body, they tend to take partial, shallow breaths that provide enough oxygen for survival, but little more.

Of course, we cannot be conscious of our breathing patterns all day long, but the good news is that we don't need to be. If we simply pause two or three times a day and focus on breathing effectively for a minute or so, we will soon notice an improvement in our energy levels, our ability to concentrate, and even on our emotional outlook.

What exactly does the term 'breathing effectively' mean? For our purposes, it means taking a slow, deep inhalation to the count of four and allowing the abdomen to extend. Then hold the breath for a count of four before exhaling slowly and fully for a count of four whilst bringing the abdomen back in. Repeat this process ten or twenty times at each session, two or three times each day, and you will soon notice the difference.

Eliminate poisons from your system

Despite the fact that modern society is supposed to be so health-conscious, many people routinely poison their physical bodies with all manner of harmful substances. Some people smoke cigarettes, some smoke cigars and others drink alcohol to excess. All of these poisons, regardless of whether they work as stimulants in the short term, actually decrease the amount of energy a person has over the long term.

If you want to increase your physical energy levels you need to eliminate such poisons from your system – starting immediately. Quit smoking in any form and reduce the consumption of alcohol to a bare minimum. Of course, this is very easy to say in one sentence, and I understand that quitting any of these things tests your willpower to the limit; but if you obtain as much support as you need – for example, by obtaining nicotine patches and joining a local smoking cessation group – and you commit to following through, you will find the strength required to succeed.

Adopt a healthy diet

We looked at the details of a healthy diet in Chapter 7. Back then, we were considering the diet of your kids, but you too need to watch what you eat. As far as possible, start adhering to the guidelines outlined earlier, and remember the key point made:

A healthy diet is a common sense balance between proteins and good carbohydrates. It is rich in fruits, vegetables and fibre and low in salt, sugar, saturated fats and artificial additives.

If you adjust your diet so that it meets this healthy criterion, you will discover that your energy levels improve and become a lot more stable throughout each day.

Take regular exercise

Again, this is something that we discussed in an earlier chapter, but let's pause for a moment to examine how exercise relates to physical energy. Far too many people say that they don't exercise because they don't have the energy. The fact is that those who exercise on a regular basis find that their energy levels actually increase – and if you recall what I said about the role of oxygen a little while ago, this shouldn't be surprising.

Of course, if you haven't exercised for a while then you will probably need to discipline yourself to do so. The good news is that, if you persist, exercise will actually become more and more enjoyable, thanks to the increase in feel-good chemicals that occurs naturally in the brain during periods of aerobic activity.

Principle 3: Manage your stress level

Stress is a normal part of life, and no matter who we are or what we do, we can never totally eliminate it from our experience. We can, however, learn to gain more control over the way we react to life so that we keep the negative effects of stress to a minimum. Although physical exercise is also a very good tool in this respect, one of the best ways to manage your stress level is to learn the discipline of daily meditation.

If you're beginning to worry about wearing orange robes or chanting in a corner, relax. Meditation is simply a mental exercise that is scientifically proven to calm the body as well as the mind. When practised regularly, it helps to reduce your stress level and lower your blood pressure, and it can even assist in overcoming physical addictions such as smoking.

Beginning a daily meditation practice is very simple. To start, find a quiet place where you will not be disturbed. Sit on the floor, on a cushion or in a chair and close your eyes. Take a few deep breaths and allow your body to relax. Keep your spine as straight as you can and allow your hands to rest in your lap or on the knees.

Now focus your entire attention on your breathing. 'Watch' the breath as it enters your nostrils on every inhalation, then as it leaves on every exhalation. If you wish, you can count the breaths, counting 'one' for the inhalation, 'two' for the exhalation, 'three' for the next inhalation, and so on, starting all over again when the count reaches ten.

Continue doing this for around twenty to thirty minutes, and aim to keep your focus on your breathing for the entire duration. This is an ability that comes with practice, and at first you will probably find it quite difficult to keep your mind focused. Instead, other thoughts might creep into your mind. You might suddenly remember a deadline you have to meet, a bill you need to pay or a promise you have yet to keep. Whatever distractions occur, ignore them and return attention to your breathing.

When you end your meditation session, don't simply jump up and get back to the business of living. Take a few slow, deep breaths, open your eyes and allow the calm of the meditation to stay with you as you return to your normal duties.

The benefits of meditation are largely cumulative. This means that you can't expect to meditate just once and bring your stress level down to a minimum. You need to meditate daily, preferably twice a day, and allow the benefits to come as gradually as they want to come. If you do this then you will find that, after several months, meditation becomes something that enhances your life far more than you currently imagine.

Principle 4: Maintain your romantic relationship

The fourth way to meet your needs as a man is to consciously work to maintain your romantic relationship with your partner. It is very easy for both parents to forget that they had a fulfilling relationship long before any children arrived on the scene, and unless you deliberately plan to keep this original relationship going, you could well end up living more like flatmates than lovers.

It is obviously more difficult to be romantic when there are kids around than it was previously, but it's by no means impossible. Here are some ways you can maintain your romantic relationship over the coming years:

- Spend time alone together. If you have introduced regular bedtimes for your children, you should be able to set aside at least one night a week to focus on your romantic relationship. Although scheduling such things might sound a little mechanical, it is by far the best approach to take if you want to keep the relationship thriving.

- Treat your partner as a woman. When you are alone with your partner, treat her as a woman, and not simply as a mother. She will be feeling like a mother all day long, so help her to break out of the role whenever the kids are safely tucked up in bed by viewing her as a person, rather than a job description.

- Arrange to go out as a couple. Do this at least once a month without the kids. You may need to call on the help of relatives to baby-sit, but this is rarely a problem. Getting out of the house without having to worry about what Junior is doing – whether it's for an evening meal at a restaurant or a good lunch at a local steak-house – is not usually a difficult thing to do – but it is something that will make both of you feel good.

- Give yourselves privacy. As kids get older, they may get more intrusive. If you need to, put a small lock or a chain on your bedroom door to ensure that you will both be able to relax without worrying about privacy issues.

- Take care of yourself. Many men settle down and then let themselves go, but only a few will ever admit it to themselves. Be as conscious of your appearance and manners now as you were when you first met your partner and you won't go far wrong.

Thinking of their own needs is something that many great dads forget to do, but it's essential for long-term effectiveness. By looking after yourself in the ways suggested, you will be in far better shape to look after those you love.

Summary of Chapter 17

- If you want to be a truly great dad, you need to make sure that you pay attention to your own needs as well as those of everyone else. There are several simple ways to do this.
- Principle 1: Make time for yourself.
- Principle 2: Increase your physical energy levels by:
  - deep breathing
  - eliminating poisons from your system
  - adopting a healthy diet
  - taking regular exercise.
- Principle 3: Manage your stress level with meditation.
- Principle 4: Maintain your romantic relationship by:
  - spending time alone together
  - treating your partner as a woman, and not simply a mother
  - arranging to go out as a couple at least once a month without the kids
  - giving yourselves privacy
  - taking care of your appearance and manners.

The Great Dad's First Aid Kit

Sometimes it's hard being a great dad, and no matter how great you are, there will always be the risk of something taking you by surprise. A daughter gets pregnant. A son starts experimenting with drugs. There are many possibilities and you can't possibly plan in advance for them all, so this chapter will serve as a virtual 'first aid kit' that you can turn to in times of crisis.

Because it's designed as a first aid kit, this chapter is not one that you have to read through in its entirety unless you want to do so. You can just as easily read through the first part, which provides brief guidance on handling a crisis effectively, and then refer to the rest of the chapter as and when needed. Do this by locating the heading that is most applicable to the situation you face and then consulting the text associated with that heading.

As well as providing basic instructions for handling a specific type of situation, each section also gives details of support systems you can turn to for additional help and advice. Remember, calling in reserve support at a time of crisis isn't a sign of weakness. It's the sign of a great dad who'll do whatever is necessary to help his kids live great lives.

With that said, let's get started ...

Handling a crisis effectively

For our purposes, a crisis can be defined as any event that threatens the mental, emotional or physical well-being of your child. This definition therefore includes everything from grieving over the death of a loved one right through to indulging in sexual activity before the age of sixteen. Despite this enormous diversity, there are several steps that you can take to help your child no matter what type of crisis he or she faces.

Step 1: Identify the crisis

In many cases, the most difficult aspect of handling a crisis is being able to identify that one exists in the first place. Of course, this isn't a problem when the cause is obvious, such as the death of a loved one; but when the cause is less obvious, kids are often quite secretive about their situation. This is usually because the child is scared of how the parents might react (as in the case of a teenage girl who suspects she is pregnant), or because he or she really doesn't recognise the situation as being a problem in the first place (as in the case of a teenage boy who likes to spray paint on bus shelters with his friends at the weekends).

A major key to identifying a crisis is to know what to look for. If you are conscious of how your child behaves when everything is going well, you are much more likely to notice a sudden change in behaviour that might indicate a problem. Although every child is different, there are several 'warning signs' that are often observed at times of crisis, and knowing about these is always useful. The signs include:

- sudden emotional outbursts, ranging from screaming and shouting to crying for no apparent reason
- loss of appetite
- loss of interest in activities that are usually enjoyed
- sudden withdrawal from, and/or a marked decrease in, communication with friends and other family members.

Any of these things taken alone are fairly common in kids, especially when they are coming down with a physical illness such as the flu, so don't always think CRISIS! every time your child refuses dessert. However, if several of the above signs are observed, and you are confident that your child isn't physically ill, the chances are that there is a problem that needs to be dealt with.

Step 2: Communicate

Once you are fairly certain that there is a crisis taking place on some level, the next step is to communicate with your child so that he or she opens up and discusses it with you. This isn't always easy, because your child might be feeling guilty or fearful of your reaction to whatever it is he or she is wrestling with. You can usually encourage them to open up by giving certain assurance, along these lines:

- Problems are always less formidable when they are shared, but can often seem impossible to solve when kept to oneself.

- Simply hoping that a problem will solve itself over time usually results in the problem getting worse. The only way to get through a crisis or overcome a problem is to face it and take whatever action is necessary.

- You are on the same side, and even if you disagree with your child's actions or perspectives you will do your best to help solve whatever problem or issue he or she is facing.

Step 3: Be proactive and solutions-oriented

Although you may be tempted to give your child a hard time about the current problem, this won't exactly encourage them to be open with you in the future. Instead, step back from your own emotional reaction so that you can address the problem itself with a proactive and solutions-oriented approach.

With some problems, such as teen pregnancy and substance abuse, you yourself may need further guidance from a reliable and non-judgemental source. To help you obtain this guidance you will find the names and contact details of relevant support groups in the subject-specific sections later in this chapter.

Even if a problem cannot literally be 'solved' (as in the case of a bereavement), you can still take a proactive approach that focuses on dealing with the situation as positively and practically as possible. For example, you can encourage a grieving child to get back to a more normal routine, and so on. Taking positive action of any sort will almost always help a child to feel less daunted by a difficult situation.

Step 4: Encourage your child to learn from the experience

Whatever the exact nature of the crisis, encourage your child to learn something from the whole experience. By doing this you will be teaching that even tough situations can provide useful lessons in life that can be beneficial in the future.

First aid for common crisis situations

Bereavement

At some point in life we all have to deal with the death of a friend or loved one and go through the painful process of grieving. For a child, bereavement is a particularly challenging experience and involves all sorts of emotions, including fear, denial, loneliness, regret, heartbreak, a feeling of being abandoned and an inappropriate sense of guilt.

It is important that you give support through the grieving process – even if they are only grieving over the death of a pet goldfish – and that you reassure the child that they are not to blame in any way. Teach that death is a fact of life, and that although it is always unpleasant for those who are left behind, it is something we all have to learn to deal with.

Teach your kids that the best way of showing their love for someone who has died is by living their own life as fully as they can, but don't expect them to act on this perspective immediately. Grieving takes time, so allow them to go through the process properly and be sure to remind them that you are there to love and support them all the way.

For further information and support, contact
ChildLine: 0800 11 11

Launched in 1986, ChildLine has counselled well over one million children and young people and has ten counselling centres around the UK. This charitable organisation provides information and advice on a variety of topics directly to children. The service runs 24 hours a day, 7 days a week, all year round.

Depression and anxiety

When most people think of psychological problems such as depression and anxiety, they tend to assume that these are exclusive to adults. But they're wrong. Kids can get as depressed, hyperactive or anxious as the rest of us, and although their moods often improve over time, when the problem is ongoing it's a good idea to ensure that they aren't suffering from a physiological or mental health disorder.

It's important that we know this, because if a genuine disorder is at work, no amount of urging a child to 'pull yourself together' will have an effect. On the contrary, if your child feels bad and doesn't know why, he or she will simply feel guilty about not being able to 'sort myself out' as dad suggests.

Your first port of call should be with your general practitioner, who will begin by assessing the physical health of your child. Sometimes moods are affected by underlying health problems, so it's important to check this out before going further. If there are no physical reasons for the depression or anxiety, the GP will then decide whether the problem is worthy of referral to someone who specialises in child psychology. Seeing a mental health professional about a mood disorder is no more unusual than seeing a dietician about a weight problem, so if this is deemed necessary, be sure to take the route your doctor suggests.

For further information and support, contact
Young Minds: 0800 018 2138

YoungMinds is a national charity that exists to improve the mental health of children and young people. The telephone number given above will connect you to their Parents' Information Service which provides advice for anyone concerned about the mental health of a child or young person. The organisation also produces a variety of leaflets and publications to help both parents and kids find the relevant information and support they require.

Drug and substance abuse

Drug and substance abuse is becoming increasingly common in the UK. Whether it's smoking weed, sniffing glue or taking ecstasy at a party, kids are putting their health at risk far more often than most parents imagine.

Kids experiment with drugs for the same reasons that adults drink or smoke – either because they want to change the way they feel or because they want to 'fit in' with their friends who are doing the same. It's therefore important to educate your child about drugs and their dangers rather than simply hope that the subject won't crop up.

If you discover that your child has been taking drugs – either illegal ones such as cannabis or legal ones such as alcohol – you need to have a serious talk about the consequences. Don't just say that 'drugs can kill' but really explore the issues as fully as your child is able to understand. In this situation, obtaining further information and support is essential.

For further information and support, contact
Frank: 0800 77 66 00

The Frank campaign is jointly funded by the Home Office and the Department of Health, working closely with the Department for Education and Skills, and centres on providing young people with credible and reliable information to understand the risks associated with drug use. It also gives parents and carers the skills and confidence to communicate with their children about drugs, raising awareness of the risks associated with drug use and providing a source of advice, information and support. Staffed by trained specialists, the helpline provides the facts on drugs and refers callers to treatment and support organisations.

Eating disorders

It is a common assumption that eating disorders are a relatively recent problem, but the fact is that both anorexia nervosa and bulimia nervosa have been around for centuries. They were named as clinical conditions in 1873 and 1979 respectively.

Anorexia nervosa is an eating disorder that, according to the World Health Organisation, 'is characterised by deliberate weight loss, induced and/or sustained by the patient'. It is most common in adolescent girls and young women, though boys, men and women of all other ages can also be affected. Initially, the condition can be observed as an overwhelming desire to be thinner, and this tends to result in dietary restrictions and/or an increase in exercise to burn off 'excess' calories. However, if these strict attitudes continue, actual chemical changes can take place in both the physiological and neurological systems, making recovery extremely difficult. If left untreated, anorexia nervosa can result in death.

Bulimia nervosa is another eating disorder that, according to the World Health Organisation, 'is characterised by repeated bouts of overeating and an excessive preoccupation with the control of body weight, leading the patient to adopt extreme measures so as to mitigate the "fattening" effects of ingested food'. These extreme measures include causing oneself to vomit, taking laxatives or doing both. There is no single reason why anyone should suffer from such eating disorders, though there can be 'trigger incidents' which mark their onset.

All eating disorders require medical attention and intervention, so if your child ever admits 'binging and purging' or diets excessively, it is a good idea to talk the matter through with your GP in the first instance.

For further information and support, contact
Eating Disorders Association: 01603 621414 (Helpline)
or 01603 765050 (Youthline)

The Eating Disorders Association is a national charity providing information, help and support for people affected by eating disorders, especially anorexia and bulimia.

Pregnancy

Experimentation with sexuality among kids is even more common than experimentation with drugs, and this naturally means that some girls under the age of sixteen become pregnant. Non-consensual intercourse is obviously a police matter and should be reported immediately. If your child admits to having had full consensual intercourse, then resist any urge to judge or criticise and focus on taking supportive action. A pregnancy test is essential, but visiting your GP is a much better option than using a home-testing kit because of the more complex psychological and practical implications of a teen pregnancy.

If your child is not actually pregnant, you should sit down and discuss sex with her in a very practical way. Remind her of the legal position on underage sex and of the benefits of abstinence. But also provide plenty of information on contraception just in case she decides to continue having sex anyway. Providing her with the contact details of Sexwise (see below) might also be a good idea.

If your daughter is pregnant then obviously the situation is even more complex. You will need to help her make some very difficult decisions, and you will probably need some support yourself – so follow up any recommendations given by your GP and also consult the fpa (see below).

For further information and support, contact
Sexwise: 0800 28 29 30

Sexwise is an independent charity helpline that offers anyone under the age of eighteen free, confidential advice on sex, relationships and contraception. The freephone helpline is open from 7am to midnight, every day of the week, and they don't ask for the caller's name at any time during the call.

For further information and support, contact
fpa: 0845 310 1334

Formerly known as the Family Planning Association, the fpa is the only registered charity working to improve the sexual health and reproductive rights of all people throughout the UK. This organisation can be of help both to your child and to you as a parent, so be sure to make yourself aware of the information and services it provides.

SUMMARY OF CHAPTER 18

Sometimes it's hard being a great dad, and no matter how great you are, there will always be the risk of something taking you by surprise.

Despite the enormous diversity of problems that could potentially crop up, there are several steps that you can take to help your child no matter what type of crisis he or she faces.

- Step 1: Identify the crisis.
- Step 2: Communicate and assure your child that:
  - Problems are always less formidable when they are shared, but can often seem impossible to solve when kept to oneself.
  - Simply hoping that a problem will solve itself over time usually results in the problem getting worse. The only way to get through a crisis or overcome a problem is to face it and take whatever action is necessary.
  - You are on their side, and even if you disagree with their actions or perspectives, you will do your best to help them solve whatever problem or issue they face.
- Step 3: Be proactive and solutions-oriented.
- Step 4: Encourage your child to learn something from the experience.

CHAPTER 19

Living Apart

In earlier chapters we have assumed that you will be living with your partner and child and therefore working at being a great dad 'on site'. Whilst this assumption holds good for many fathers, a growing number are having to adjust to living apart from their kids following a divorce or separation. Although living apart presents more problems than living together (because of access rules and so on) it's still perfectly possible to be a great dad if you go about things in the right way. There are a number of basic principles that we can consider to help you in this area.

Eight basic principles

Principle 1: Understand the emotional consequences of separation and divorce

It is never easy to divorce or separate, and everyone concerned will experience all sorts of painful emotions. For fathers, it often leads to 'grieving' the loss of continual contact with their children, and the range of emotions experienced here tends to follow the same pattern as experienced by those who are coming to terms with any other major loss. Understanding this pattern will help you to view your current position in a larger context, and will therefore help you to see light at the end of the tunnel.

First, you will be emotionally affected by the absence of your kids. You may want to cry, shout, scream or lash out at something or someone. The best way to get through this stage is to actually allow yourself to cry, or to take yourself to a secluded beach and scream and shout. If you feel like lashing out, go to the gym and pound a punch-bag or take your aggression out on a weights machine. You will recover much faster by allowing yourself to release these emotions than you would if you were to try to suppress them.

After this initial wave of emotion, most fathers feel angry or resentful towards other people who can be 'blamed' for the situation – usually the ex-partner or the legal system that determined custody and access rules. Whilst such anger is understandable, you need to remember that trying to buck the system or break the rules will only make matters worse for you. The best way to handle this phase of emotion is to choose to be the best father you possibly can be within the parameters of the law, and to prove that you are stronger than the circumstances that are testing you.

The final stage commonly experienced is one of acceptance. This is when you finally accept the new situation and are therefore ready to move on to living your life in a different way. Rather than being concerned about what used to be the norm, you focus on what is the norm right now, and you strive to make the most of it.

Principle 2: Be involved as much as you can

Although there may be restrictions on the amount of access you have to your kids, you should be involved in their lives as much as you can. Support them at school by attending sports days, Christmas concerts and football or netball matches. If you can, attend parent meetings. Take advantage of every opportunity to see your children and you can be confident that you are – as far as possible – doing everything within your ability to give your relationship with your kids the time and attention it deserves.

Principle 3: Don't rely on support from your former partner

Even if the decision to separate or divorce was amicable, you shouldn't expect continued support from your ex-partner. This is not to say that you won't get support, but simply that you shouldn't rely on it. The sooner you start living as a single, independent man, the better it will be for you and for your children.

Principle 4: Create an alternative support network

Don't think that you don't need any support at all, because you do. Creating an alternative support network by strengthening old friendships is always a good idea, and will help you to enjoy those aspects of life that don't involve your kids. Joining a local support organisation which specifically exists for fathers living apart from their kids is also a very good idea. If no local group exists, consider contacting one of the following national organisations.

For further information and support, contact
Dads UK: 07092 391489 or 07092 390210

This is not an organisation that provides group meetings, but a helpline for single fathers. The helpline is open Monday to Friday from 11am to 10pm, and at weekends between 2–6pm.

For further information and support, contact
Families Need Fathers: 0870 760 7496

This is a social care organisation that believes that parents should be of equal status in law. It provides books, leaflets, a website, a telephone helpline and Internet forums which members can use to share support and advice. Call the number given between 6pm and 10pm.

Principle 5: Parent for the best interests of your child

A common mistake among separated parents is parenting for the sake of scoring 'points' against the other parent. For example, a mother might forbid fast food, so the father takes his kids to an 'all you can eat' meal at the local pizza house. Such a move will probably help him to become more popular with his child, but this popularity is only temporary, and by no means in anyone's best interests long term.

Your role as a great dad doesn't change just because you live apart from your kids. Your job is still to be the best dad you possibly can be, even if that means coming second in the popularity stakes. Whilst you are with your kids, provide the same high standard of parenting that you would give if you weren't living apart.

Principle 6: Promote healthy relationships all round

Although you no longer live with your ex-partner, your child should still grow up to love and respect you both. You should be careful to speak sensibly about your ex-partner whilst with your child, and you should encourage your child to treat the mother with the same kind of respect shown to you. The problem with using kids as 'pawns' in battles between ex-partners is that the kids suffer and nobody derives any benefit. By deliberately promoting healthy relationships all round, you are much more likely to keep the communication channels open with your ex-partner – and this will naturally result in a more stable situation for all concerned.

Principle 7: Don't sweat the small stuff

When you lived with your partner, you had a right to be involved in every aspect of your child's life, from the choice of breakfast cereal to the time he or she went to bed at night. This changes when you live apart, and you may need to get used to stepping back from things that you don't agree with. The easiest way of doing this is to adopt the motto of American author Richard Carlson: 'Don't Sweat the Small Stuff'. In other words, learn to ignore trivial matters that you might have disagreed about previously, and challenge your ex-partner only on things that are really important, such as the choice of school or rules on the limits of acceptable behaviour. This approach will make your life a lot less stressful than if you were to challenge everything your ex-partner does.

Principle 8: Communicate with your ex on a regular basis

If she's willing, it is a good idea to set up a routine of communicating with your ex-partner on a regular basis (such as once a fortnight or once a month) so that you can sit down and discuss your child's life and progress and make important decisions together. This might not sound like a lot of fun, especially if you parted on less than amicable terms. But if you can both put aside your personal differences in order to focus on the well-being of your kids, you will find that life as a father living apart becomes a great deal easier.

Whilst a complete guide to parenting after a divorce or separation is beyond the scope of this book, these eight basic principles should prove useful to you. However, for a more in-depth look at the subject of divorce and separation and its effects on children, I highly recommend a book entitled *How to Help the Children Survive the Divorce* by Jody Beveridge and Alan Bradley. Both these professional authors work in the areas of family support and family law and have deep experience of the cause-and-effect problems that relate to divorce

SUMMARY OF CHAPTER 19

Although living apart presents more problems than living together, it's still perfectly possible to be a great dad if you go about things in the right way. There are a number of basics to help you in this area:

- Principle 1: Understand the emotional consequences of separation and divorce.
- Principle 2: Be involved as much as the law allows you to be.
- Principle 3: Don't rely on support from your former partner.
- Principle 4: Create an alternative support network.
- Principle 5: Parent for the best interests of your child – not to score 'points'.
- Principle 6: Promote healthy relationships all round.
- Principle 7: Don't sweat the small stuff.
- Principle 8: Communicate with your ex-partner on a regular basis.

CHAPTER 20

Coping with Special Needs

'Life is what happens when you're busy making other plans.'

John Lennon

Whether we like it or not, life doesn't always go according to plan. We can make all the preparations we want for the future, but sometimes the unexpected happens and a completely different future appears before us out of thin air.

If you're the parent of a child with special needs then you'll know what I'm talking about all too well. One day you're dreaming about your 'imminent arrival' growing up to be a Premiership football player, a Nobel prize-winning rocket scientist or a female kick-boxing champion, and then your child arrives and you realise that none of these things is very likely because he or she simply isn't equipped to play football or make rocket-science breakthroughs.

Having a child with special needs presents a number of unique challenges, but it can also provide a number of unique positive experiences as well. This brief chapter explores some of the main issues for those of you who discover that, as John Lennon famously said, 'Life is what happens when you are busy making other plans.'

What are special needs?

The term 'special needs' is used to cover an extremely wide area, but in this chapter I am specifically referring to children who are born with more severe physical and/or mental conditions such as autism, blindness, deafness, spina bifida, cerebral palsy and – as in the case of my own youngest child – Down's syndrome.

We say that a child *has* special needs because this is far more accurate than using the condition itself as an identifying label. Saying that 'Johnny is spina bifida' is about as accurate as saying 'Johnny is brown hair.' It's nonsense. Johnny may *have* spina bifida and he may *have* brown hair, but at the end of the day he is simply Johnny. This might sound like nothing but semantics to those of you who are reading this chapter out of curiosity rather than because it is relevant to your own situation, but to Johnny and those who know him it really is a big deal.

Finding out

Although routine screening during pregnancy does help doctors to diagnose that some children have special needs before they are born, in many cases nobody is aware of the situation until the baby is actually born. If a medical professional suspects that your newborn has special needs (it isn't always obvious by any means) then he or she will be examined further so that a definite diagnosis can be made as soon as possible. Doctors always try to break the news to parents as gently as they can, but it always comes as a shock, and parents react in a variety of different ways. Some are horrified, some get angry and look for someone to blame (even if it's themselves), some break down in tears, some deny that there is anything wrong, and some take the news in their stride.

There is no 'right' or 'wrong' way to react to this kind of news, but there are several things that you can bear in mind to help you keep things in perspective if you ever receive it.

- *You aren't alone.* There are far more kids with special needs in the world than you currently realise, so don't think that you're the only couple experiencing this.

- *It isn't all bad news.* There are thousands of other parents in this country who will back me up when I tell you that kids with special needs can enjoy very happy and fulfilling lives.

- *It isn't always difficult.* Whilst parenting a kid with special needs can undoubtedly be difficult at times, it isn't always that way. What you now think of as being difficult will eventually become relatively easy, or at least commonplace, and parenting your child will be just as much of a privilege and a joy as it is for everyone else.

- You will get plenty of support right across the board: financial support, educational support, emotional support – whatever kind of support you need.

Accepting and adapting

There are two things you can do when something unexpected happens in life. You can try to deny reality and hope that you'll soon wake up from what you hope is a bad dream, or you can accept the new situation and adapt to it. The first option leads to frustration, emotional pain and resentment. The second option enables you to move forward in a more proactive and positive frame of mind. Learning to accept the new situation and adapting yourself to it doesn't happen overnight, but it will certainly happen a lot faster if you make a conscious decision to take this healthier route forward.

Obtaining advice and support

From the moment it is confirmed that your child has a special need, you will immediately be offered all the help, guidance, advice and support you could ever hope for. It is a good idea to accept this assistance, as the early days of parenting will obviously be the most difficult as far as adjusting to the situation is concerned. The assistance offered will take various forms as your child gets older, but will typically include:

- help applying for any disability benefits your child may be entitled to

- counselling and emotional support, often including optional contact with other parents in your own area who have – like myself – 'been there and done that' and can tell you how to get the stains out of your T-shirt

- help obtaining any special items of equipment you may need, such as bed-rails, toilet seats, car and pushchair harnesses, and so on.

- ongoing medical examinations and, if necessary, treatment. Although many kids with special needs are perfectly healthy apart from their obvious 'special need', some can also have health complications that need to be assessed on a regular basis. For example, it is not uncommon for a child with Down's also to have heart problems.

- an invitation to join a general support group of parents who are in a similar situation, although probably not with the same specific 'special needs' issues as yourself. Whether you choose to join a group for the long term is entirely up to you, but most parents will benefit from at least exploring the option before making a decision.

At any point, if you need support, advice or guidance that is not automatically offered (such as answers to questions you have about the future), do not hesitate to speak up and ask for it. Although the medical profession does its best to be as 'on the ball' as possible, they aren't mind-readers and it's your responsibility to take the initiative and ask for further information or help as and when you need it.

Living with your child

Some readers may be offended by the fairly light-hearted attitude I have taken in this chapter thus far. I apologise if you are one of them, but in my own experience, having a light heart and an optimistic approach is far better than looking at the down-sides of a situation – and this applies especially to your day-to-day life.

Living with a child who has special needs is a lot like living with any other kid, but a tad more challenging at times. They want all the same things as other kids – love, support, encouragement, fun, and so on – but will need a little extra assistance in areas affected by their specific condition. A child who is blind will need you to speak and touch them more, so that they are fully aware of your presence. A child who is deaf will need you to be more conscious of your visual expressions. Apart from these case-specific 'extras', here are some rather more general principles you can follow to get the maximum joy and fulfilment from your situation:

- *Enjoy each day with your child.* Life is not about what will happen next month, next year or a decade down the line. It's about what happens today, in the present moment. Make a conscious decision to enjoy your child on a day-to-day basis, to make him or her laugh or smile on a day-to-day basis, and to share hugs and kisses on a day-to-day basis. Let them know that you love them exactly as they are.

- *Don't underestimate your child.* Although the fact that there exists a 'special need' of some sort will obviously affect your child's ability in certain areas, this doesn't mean that he or she won't be perfectly capable of excelling in other areas. We can encourage a blind child to sing and tell stories and learn Braille. We can encourage a deaf child to mime and read and learn to use a sign language. We can encourage a child with Down's to run, jump and dance. Remember at all times that a child with special needs requires just as much encouragement to do well as any other child. Whilst his or her potential may not be the same as that of some other children, your kid still needs to live up to that potential, so cheer the child on at every opportunity.

- *Don't expect a little angel.* There's a mistaken belief that a child with special needs somehow misses out on the 'naughty' gene. They don't. Kids with special needs can be as naughty as any other, and as they grow up they still need to be taught – as far as they can understand – the difference between right and wrong, and what is acceptable behaviour. Of course, kids who have delayed learning abilities will take longer to figure this stuff out, and you will probably have to be a lot more patient with their behaviour. But don't sit back and let them get their own way all the time. If you do, you'll regret it.

- *If you have more than one child, be aware of how you divide your attention between them.* I have mentioned sibling rivalry elsewhere, but it can be more of a problem in this situation for obvious reasons. Taking your children out together or playing with them together is definitely a good thing, but occasionally it is a good idea to give each of your children 100 per cent of your attention for a time so that they don't feel as though they are in competition.

- *When your child gets older, you may be offered something called 'respite care'.* This is where your child is taken care of by a professional special needs worker (or team of workers) for a time so that you and the rest of the family can have a break from the heightened responsibilities you live with every day. Some families have a couple of hours of respite care every few weeks, so that a child with special needs can be taken to a play centre or park, for example. Others have a week of respite care every year or two – in this case a child with special needs might be taken to a holiday centre or similar. How much respite care you are offered or choose to use will obviously vary according to your personal circumstances, but do consider taking advantage of this service if and when it becomes applicable to you.

Final words

Parenting a child with special needs can be as easy or as difficult as you choose to make it, and this choice is made by the mental attitude you take towards life. If you focus exclusively on all the negatives – on what your child can't do, won't be able to do and will possibly miss out on – you're going to make things very difficult for yourself. But if, after becoming aware of the negatives, you decide to focus on the positives – on what your child can do, will learn to do and will possibly be able to enjoy in the future – you will find that your parenting experience will be one that is extremely fulfilling and meaningful.

We can't control much of what happens externally, but we have total control over the way we respond to external reality. Choose an empowering attitude and you'll be giving your child the most valuable gift in the world.

SUMMARY OF CHAPTER 20

- Having a child with special needs presents a number of unique challenges, but it can also provide a number of unique positive experiences as well.

- There are several things you can bear in mind to help you keep things in perspective if you are told that your child has special needs:
  - You aren't alone.
  - It isn't all bad news.
  - It isn't always difficult.
  - You will get plenty of support right across the board.

- Learn to accept the new situation and adapt yourself to it so that you can move forward in a more proactive and positive frame of mind.

- At any point, if you need support, advice or guidance that is not automatically offered, don't hesitate to speak up and ask for it.

- There are several general principles you can follow to get the maximum joy and fulfilment from your situation:
  - Enjoy each day with your child.
  - Don't underestimate your child.
  - Don't expect a little angel.
  - If you have several kids, be aware of how you divide your attention between them.

- You can't control much of what happens externally, but you have total control over the way you respond to external reality. Choose an empowering attitude and you'll be giving your child the most valuable gift in the world.

CHAPTER 21

Miscarriage and Stillbirth

Despite the fact that miscarriage is actually quite common, few people talk about the subject, and as a result those women who experience it can feel very isolated and lonely. This brief chapter will give you some important facts about miscarriage and stillbirth, and offer suggestions on how men can support both themselves and their partners at this difficult time. I would like to thank the Miscarriage Association for their kind permission to quote directly from some of their publications in this chapter.

Some facts about miscarriage and stillbirth

Both miscarriage and stillbirth refer to the spontaneous end of a pregnancy. Miscarriage is the term used for pregnancies that end before 24 weeks, and stillbirth for those that end after 24 weeks. It is estimated that approximately 75 per cent of miscarriages take place within the first 12 weeks of pregnancy. According to the Miscarriage Association:

- More than one in five pregnancies ends in miscarriage. That equates to around a quarter of a million in the UK each year.

- Any woman who is at risk of pregnancy is also at risk of miscarriage. It can happen to anyone.

- Most women never know what has caused them to miscarry. Investigations are generally limited to women who have had three or more miscarriages. Even after investigations, in many cases a specific cause is not found.

- It is common for women who have miscarried to feel high levels of anxiety in a subsequent pregnancy.

- Even after several miscarriages, most women have a good chance of a successful pregnancy.

What are the possible causes?

As we saw a few moments ago, most women never know exactly what caused them to miscarry. However, medical experts generally agree that there are a number of possible causes, including:

- the occurrence of random genetic abnormalities

- spontaneous rejection of the placenta by the immune system

- serious illness or infection, or hormonal irregularities.

Helping yourself and your partner after a miscarriage

A miscarriage is a very real loss for both of you, and avoiding the subject or hoping that the pain will automatically heal itself isn't helpful. Here are some ideas on how you can help both yourself and your partner to heal:

- *Rest.* Your partner will need physical rest after a miscarriage, and you should support her at this time. If necessary, take a few days off work so that you both have some time to come to terms with what has happened.

- *Talk.* Although it is often tempting for men to want to withdraw and deal with their emotions on their own, sitting down and talking things through with your partner is a much better option, as this will help you both to come to terms with the situation as a couple, and can strengthen your relationship further at this difficult time.

- *Don't blame.* Miscarriages are common, and have no clear cause that can be identified automatically, so don't blame yourselves or anyone else for the loss.

- *Don't suppress or create emotions.* Some people – both men and women – grieve extensively after a miscarriage. Others feel extremely sad and disappointed. There is no right or wrong way to react, so don't try to suppress feelings of grief or create feelings of guilt because you don't think you're reacting appropriately. Simply give yourself and your partner time to deal with whatever emotions you experience as they arise.

- *Obtain support.* If you want support or someone to speak to, turn to a local group or contact the Miscarriage Association.

- *Have hope.* Although it is obviously very difficult to be optimistic about the future following a miscarriage, try to remember that the chances of the next pregnancy progressing to full term are actually very good.

The Miscarriage Association

The Miscarriage Association respond swiftly and sympathetically to around 15,000 calls, e-mails and letters a year from those affected by the loss of a baby in pregnancy. They have a UK-wide network of over 150 volunteer telephone contacts who have been through pregnancy loss themselves and can offer support, understanding and a listening ear. Their helpline is staffed Monday to Friday from 9am to 4pm.

As well as producing leaflets, factsheets and audiotapes which answer the most commonly asked questions about pregnancy loss, the association also has 50 support groups across the UK where people can meet and share their experiences and feelings in a safe and supportive environment.

The Miscarriage Association's helpline can be contacted on 01924 200799 (in Scotland: 0131 334 8883).

SUMMARY OF CHAPTER 21

- Both miscarriage and stillbirth refer to the spontaneous ending of a pregnancy. It is estimated that about 75 per cent of miscarriages take place within the first 12 weeks of pregnancy.
- A miscarriage is a very real loss for both of you. You can help yourself and your partner to heal by:
  - ensuring that your partner gets as much physical rest as she needs
  - talking things through together
  - accepting the situation without trying to blame anyone for it
  - allowing whatever emotions you both feel to be experienced and expressed
  - obtaining support from a local group or the Miscarriage Association.
- Have hope for the future.

Afterword

Instructional books such as this one are a lot like hammers. They can be extremely valuable if we actually pick them up and use them, but they're much less valuable if all we do is put them on a shelf and look at them from a distance. Since you've gone to the trouble of not only picking this book up, but of reading right through to this afterword, I hope that you will take the final step and begin applying all that you have learned to your role as a great dad.

Being a great dad is a process, not an end goal. The longer you live, and the more you apply the principles you have discovered here, the greater you'll be. If your children one day become parents, they are more likely to be great too. Not because greatness is genetic, but simply because you've worked hard to be the role model of excellence that they need.

As you move forward, aim to live by the Eight Key Traits of Paternal Greatness that we looked at in detail way back in Chapter 1:

- The great dad gives unconditional love.

- The great dad communicates openly.

- The great dad spends time with his kids.

- The great dad is patient.

- The great dad sets a great example.

- The great dad knows how to have fun.

- The great dad provides for his children.

- The great dad is committed to greatness.

By living up to this role, and applying the principles you have read about in this book, you will discover that becoming a great dad is a lot easier than most people imagine.

Here's to your inevitable greatness!

About the Author

For over fifteen years, professional life coach and author Ian Bruce has been helping individuals all over the world to achieve their goals and experience success at the very highest levels – in their finances, careers, relationships and, of course, as parents.

All readers of *How to Be a Great Dad* can subscribe to Ian's free weekly email newsletter which explains how to be great in every area of life. You can also choose to be coached by Ian Bruce personally, either by telephone or by the new concept of email coaching for those who have a particularly awkward schedule.

For more information on either of these exciting options, visit his website at www.rational-coaching.co.uk. But before you do, take a look at testimonials received from just a few of his previous clients ...

> *'I gave Ian a lot of work because of my personal circumstances, but he was able to help me deal with anything I threw at him. We set up manageable tasks in every session, and this helped me to focus every week. We even had a few laughs, which really lifted me up! I look back on this as very positive experience which has helped me move on towards where I want to be.'*

> *'The coaching experience with Ian has been an incredibly positive and worthwhile journey. I have benefited not only from the weekly coaching sessions, but also from the change in perspective and outlook that Ian has assisted me to develop. I have no hesitation in recommending Ian as a personal coach. He is non-judgemental, non-directive,*

effective and empowering, ensuring that I as a client recognised my own potential and – more to the point – went and did something with it!'

'Outstanding. Being coached by Ian for six weeks has helped me to transform my life beyond recognition. I'm healthier, sexier, happier and making a lot more money to boot!'

Further Sources of Information

Support for dads

BBC website
Online advice on all aspects of parenting and family life
www.bbc.co.uk/parenting

Dads UK
Support for single, bereaved or gay fathers
Tel: 07092 391489 or 07092 390210
11am–10pm weekdays and 2–6pm weekends
www.dads-uk.co.uk
85A Westbourne Street, Hove, East Sussex, BN3 5PF

Department of Trade and Industry
Advice on paternity leave, working hours, childcare etc.
Tel: 020 7215 5000
www.direct.gov.uk/Audiences/Parents/fs/en
DTI Response Centre, 1 Victoria Street, London, SW1H 0ET

Divorce
Alan Bradley and Jody Beveridge, *How to Help the Children Survive the Divorce*, Foulsham, 0-572-02956-X

Family Rights Group
Advice and support for families whose children are involved with social services
Tel: 0800 731 1696 (free and confidential advice) Mon–Fri 10–12pm and 1.30–3.30pm
Email: advice@frg.org.uk
www.frg.org.uk
The Print House, 18 Ashwin Street, London, E8 3DL

Family Welfare Association
Support for poorer families, providing grants and social work advice
Tel: 020 7254 6251

Email: fwa.headoffice@fwa.org.uk
www.fwa.org.uk
501–505 Kingsland Road, London, E8 4AU

Families Need Fathers
Advice on how to keep in contact with children after a divorce
Tel: 0870 760 7496 (between 6–10pm)
www.fnf.org.uk
134 Curtain Road, London, EC2A 3AR

Fathers 4 Justice
A civil rights movement campaigning for a child's right to see both parents and grandparents
Tel: 01787 281922 (to join only – office hours)
Email: join@fathers-4-justice.org
www.fathers-4-justice.org
PO Box 7835, Sudbury, CO10 8YT (to join only)

Fathers Direct
National information centre on fatherhood
Tel: 0845 634 1328 or telephone Parentline Plus on 0808 800 2222 (advice service)
Email: mail@fathersdirect.com
www.fathersdirect.com
Herald House, Lamb's Passage, Bunhill Row, London, EC1Y 8TQ

For Parents by Parents
A UK parenting site, funded and maintained by parents
Tel: 01296 747551
Email: contributions@forparentsbyparents.com
www.forparentsbyparents.com
C/o 31 Main Street, Bishopstone, Aylesbury, Buckinghamshire, HP17 8SF

Gingerbread
Support for single parents, with advice on finding a local support group, workshops and news
Tel (freephone): 0800 018 4318:
9am–5pm Mon–Fri
www.gingerbread.org.uk

Going Back to Work
Steve Wharton, *High-vibrational Thinking: How to get back to work*, Foulsham, 0-572-03078-9
Steve Wharton, *High-vibrational Thinking: How to restore your life-work balance*, Foulsham, 0-572-03077-0

Mothers Over 40
Online advice and support for older mums and dads
www.mothersover40.com

NSPCC
Parent and family support
Helpline: 0808 800 5000
Email: help@nspcc.org.uk
www.nspcc.org.uk
Weston House, 42 Curtain Road, London, EC2A 3NH

OnDivorce
Resource for those experiencing divorce
Tel: 0906 9060250 (Speak to a specialist lawyer. £1.50 per minute. 8–10pm, 7 days a week)
www.ondivorce.co.uk

Paternity Angel
Online advice and information from pregnancy to birth
www.paternityangel.com

Single Fathers Online
Online support and forum for single fathers
www.singlefathersonline.com

Single Parents
Online community with information, advice, first hand experiences and details of local groups
www.singleparents.org.uk

Working Families
Information for working families and employers
Tel: 020 7253 7243
Email: office@workingfamilies.org.uk
www.workingfamilies.org.uk
1–3 Berry Street, London, EC1V 0AA

Support for children and young people

Bullying
Steve Wharton, *High-vibrational Thinking: How to stop that bully*, Foulsham, 0-572-03075-4

Childline
Confidential advice
Tel: 0800 1111 (24-hour free helpline)
www.childline.org.uk

Frank
Confidential drug information and advice
Tel: 0800 77 66 00 (free and confidential 24 hours a day, 7 days a week)
Textphone: FRANK 0800 917 8765
Email: frank@talktofrank.com
www.talktofrank.com

Mental Health Foundation
Support for those with learning disabilities and mental health problems in Scotland
Tel: 0141 572 0246
Email: scotland@mhf.org.uk
www.mentalhealth.org.uk
5th Floor, Merchants House, 30 George Square, Glasgow, G2 1EG

MIND
Mental health charity based in England and Wales
Tel: 0845 766 0163
Email: contact@mind.org.uk
www.mind.org.uk
15–19 Broadway, London, E15 4BQ (England)
3rd Floor, Quebec House, Castlebridge, 5–19 Cowbridge Road East, Cardiff, CF11 9AB (Wales)

Young Minds
Mental health support for the young
Tel: 0800 018 2138 (Young Minds
Parents' information service)
www.youngminds.org.uk
102–108, Clerkenwell Road, London,
EC1H 5SA

Health matters

Alcoholics Anonymous
Advice and supporting regarding alcohol
Tel (local rates / 24 hours) 0845 769 7555
www.alcholics-anonymous.org.uk (UK)
www.alcoholics-anonymous.org (US)

Eating Disorders Association
Information and support regarding eating
disorders
Youthline: 0845 634 7650 (callers aged
18 and under)
Mon–Fri: 4–6.30pm
Sat: 1–4.30pm
Email: talkback@edauk.com
Adult helpline: 0845 634 1414
Mon–Fri: 8.30–8.30pm
Sat: 1–4.30pm
Email: helpmail@edauk.com
www.edauk.com
103 Prince of Wales Road, Norwich
NR1 1DW

Focus Adolescent Services
Advice regarding alcohol
Helpline (US only) 410-341-4216
Mon–Fri 9–5pm
www.focusas.com/Alcohol/html

Miscarriage Association
Support for those who have suffered
pregnancy loss
Tel: 01924 200 799 (Mon–Fri 9am–4pm)
0131 334 8883 (Scotland only –
answerphone with names of contacts)
C/o Clayton Hospital, Northgate,
Wakefield, West Yorkshire, WF1 3JS

NHS Direct
Advice and information
Tel: 0845 46 47
www.nhsdirect.nhs.uk

Samaritans
Confidential emotional support
National UK telephone number: 08457
90 90 90 (available 23 hours a day,
7 days a week)
Email: jo@samaritans.org (24 hours)
www.samaritans.org.uk
Write to: Chris, PO Box 90 90, Stirling,
FK8 2SA

Tips for teens

Advice regarding alcohol
www.health.org/govpubs/ph323

Sexual issues

fpa
Family Planning Association
Tel: 0845 310 1334 (low-cost national UK
helpline)
www.fpa.org.uk

Illustrated guide to growing up for
children aged 8–14
Robie. H. Harris, *Let's Talk About Sex*,
Walker Books, 1-844-28174-4

Sexwise
Free, confidential advice
Tel: 0800 28 29 30
www.ruthinking.co.uk

Healthy eating

Catherine Atkinson, *Start Right Baby and
Toddler Meal Planning*, Foulsham, 0-572-
02974-8

Anita Bean, *Healthy Eating for Kids*, A & C
Black, 0-713-66917-9

Nicola Graimes, *Brain Foods for Kids*,
Carroll & Brown Publishers Ltd,
1-903-25893-6

Ellen Shanley and Colleen Thompson,
Fueling the Teen Machine, Bull Publishing,
0-923-52157-7

Peter Vaughan, *Simply Better Food for your Baby and Children*, Foulsham, 0-572-03003-7

UK government guidelines
www.food.gov.uk/healthiereating

Magazines

Baby's Best Buys
A guide for new parents with regards to baby equipment
Quarterly £2.95

Bounty Guide to Fatherhood
Practical advice and information
Annual
Free
www.bounty.com

Dad
Magazine for new fathers
Quarterly £2

Expecting our Baby
Advice on pregnancy, birth and children up to one year of age, focuses on product testing and life experience
Monthly £2.30

Having Babies
A guide from fertility to child's first day at school
Weekly £1.75

Junior
Articles aimed at parents with children aged 0–8 years
Monthly £2.50

Online Dad magazines
www.dadsmagazine.com
www.fathermag.com
www.InteractiveDad.com
www.fqmagazine.co.uk

Parent Talk
Focuses on education, health and environment issues from a family perspective
Monthly £11 per year

Practical Parenting
Monthly magazine with articles on parenting, baby and childcare, health, children's activities and education
Monthly £2.10

Pregnancy
Articles on health, lifestyle and labour for parents
6 issues per year £2.50

The Bounty Young Family Guide
A practical, textbook-style reference guide with regards to health, nutrition and development in babies and infants
Bi-annual
www.bounty.com

Time Out Kids Out
A listings magazine for Londoners on what to see, do and where to go in and around London
11 issues per year £2.25

Clubs and entertainment

Beavers, Cubs, Scouts and Explorer Scouts
Tel: 020 8433 7292
www.scouts.org.uk

Blue Kangaroo
Family restaurant and play centre
Tel: 020 7371 7622
www.thebluekangaroo.co.uk
555, Kings Road, London, SW6 2EB

Rainbows, Brownies and Guides
Tel: 0800 1 69 59 01 (to join)
www.girlguiding.org.uk

Tumbletots
Play gym for toddlers
Tel: 0121 585 7003 for details of your
nearest group
Email: info@tumbletots.com
www.tumbletots.com

General

Citizens Advice Bureau
Telephone directory enquiries for local
numbers
www.adviceguide.org.uk

Helplines
A directory of all helplines in the UK
www.helplines.org.uk

Yellow Pages
www.yell.com (UK)
www.yellowbook.com (USA)

Index